W9-AGH-908

# Off the Record

# Off the Record

My Dream Job at the White House,
How I Lost It, and What I Learned

### MADELEINE WESTERHOUT

CENTER
STREET®

NEW YORK   NASHVILLE

Center Street
Hachette Book Group
1290 Avenue of the Americas, New York, NY 10104
centerstreet.com
twitter.com/centerstreet

First Edition: August 2020

Center Street is a division of Hachette Book Group, Inc. The Center Street
name and logo are trademarks of Hachette Book Group, Inc.

The publisher is not responsible for websites (or their content) that are
not owned by the publisher.

The Hachette Speakers Bureau provides a wide range of authors for
speaking events. To find out more, go to www.HachetteSpeakersBureau.com
or call (866) 376-6591.

*Print book interior design by Timothy Shaner, NightandDayDesign.biz*

Library of Congress Cataloging-in-Publication Data has been applied for.

ISBNs: 978-1-5460-5970-7 (hardcover), 978-1-5460-5968-4 (ebook)

Printed in the United States of America

LSC-C

10   9   8   7   6   5   4   3   2   1

*To Mom and Dad,*
*who have always supported me unconditionally*

# Contents

# Off the Record

★

# CHAPTER ONE

# The Dinner

The answer was no.

The answer was always no whenever I was asked to engage with reporters, and it didn't matter what the context was.

So naturally when I was invited to join a group of them for dinner one night in August 2019, I said no again. I had every reason to be wary.

After all, what good could possibly come of it?

Reporters are . . . reporters. They are not your friends. They care about the story, not you.

Especially the reporters who cover the Trump White House, where I worked, a White House that has been under siege from the Fourth Estate since Donald Trump took the oath of office as president. Heck, since November 2016, when the candidate the media was pulling for, Hillary Rodham Clinton, lost.

Here we are, four years later, and many Democrats still argue that Hillary should be president because she collected the most popular votes. Nonsense. A candidate wins the election by collecting the most electoral votes, and that's what Donald Trump did.

To be fair, I have no interest in indicting the entire profession. I've met my share of journalists who approach every assignment with an open mind, and don't allow their bias to slant their reporting. I understand why the president gets angry with them—there is a ton of fake news—though I don't entirely agree with him that the mainstream media are the "Enemy of the People."

Too many reporters, however, search only for evidence to back up the premise they begin with, and if finding it requires them to rely on anonymous sources or ignore irrefutable facts on the opposite side, so be it. The way they see it, any tactics, no matter how unethical, can be justified if they might lead to the downfall of the man they despise.

No president, at least in modern times, has been treated with more disrespect than Donald Trump.

Reporters claim that all they are interested in is telling the truth. Give me a break. They write their story first, act as judge and jury, and worry about the truth later. When they make a mistake, which is too often the case, good luck getting them to admit it.

The story is on the front page, impossible to miss. The correction is buried on an inside page—if it's there at all.

I can't tell you how many times I'd be sitting at my desk right outside the Oval Office and see "breaking news" about the president or somebody else in the administration on the screen and think, *Oh, my God, I can't believe this is happening*, only to find out from others in the West Wing that the report was a total fabrication.

Yet if someone like myself, who worked in the West Wing, could be misled that easily, what about the people outside of Washington who wouldn't be able to separate fact from fiction?

What bothered me more than anything was the constant stories that the president was angry the whole day, berating his aides. I had been with him from practically the moment he stepped into the Oval Office, and I can assure you that wasn't the case. Where the media came up with lies like that was beyond me.

So you can understand why I might not have been interested in having dinner with those "truth tellers."

Besides, I was enjoying a much-needed rest on a gorgeous Saturday afternoon, lounging by the pool at the president's golf club in Bedminster, New Jersey, roughly an hour from New York. Bedminster had been our home for the prior nine days. I wrote some emails, splashed around in the pool, soaked up the summer sun, and downed a few drinks.

The president always urged the staff to take advantage of the facilities at his properties once our work was done. We didn't need much convincing.

I was in a tremendous mood. Our trip in mid-August 2019 couldn't have gone any more smoothly.

The president was happy. The first lady was happy. The senior staff was happy. As his executive assistant—think Mrs. Landingham from *The West Wing*—I took a great deal of pride in what we accomplished. I was aware of how easily it could have gone the other way.

Donald Trump, you see, never looks forward to being away from the White House for more than a couple of days. He is frustrated by the image of him that has been spread by the press—shocking, I know—that he doesn't work very hard. Add that to its long list of lies. He works extremely hard. I'll go as far as to say that he has more energy than everyone else in the West Wing. We could barely keep up with him.

The president often starts his workday about 6:00 a.m.—he typically sleeps for only four or five hours—and some nights, he doesn't get off the phone until around midnight. He believes in returning everyone's call, and I mean everyone. I can't imagine there has been anyone in that office who has made himself more available.

Furthermore, he adores everything about the White House. Which is why it is outrageous that people suggest he doesn't enjoy being president. He enjoys it very much.

This is someone who didn't need the job, who took it on only because he loves his country and believed he was the right man to turn things around. He could have gone on as the celebrity he had been for much of his adult life, admired for the most part, and no one would have given it a second thought.

Instead, he ran for president, the most demanding job in the world, against overwhelming odds and put his legacy on the line.

The history of the institution itself is never lost on him. When he had a guest in the Oval Office, he often told me, "Madeleine, get the picture of John-John." He was referring to the famous photo from the early 1960s of President John F. Kennedy's two-year-old son, John-John, playing under the Resolute Desk.

"This is the same desk," President Trump would proceed to tell his guest. "Come, let's take a picture behind it."

On more than a few occasions, when some of the staff were staying a little later than usual, the president would usher us into the Oval Office. "Look around," he'd tell us. "Look where we are. How incredible is this? We are standing in the Oval Office!"

I can't overstate how much moments like that meant to me. My colleagues and I would get so wrapped up in our day-to-day responsibilities, we would forget where we were and how essential our work was. Incredibly, it was our boss, the president of the United States, who had to be the one to remind us.

He always appreciated how fortunate he was to be a part of history. I will never forget the first time the president rode on Marine One, the presidential helicopter.

From my office overlooking the Rose Garden, I watched him as he watched the helicopter land and then as he made his way from the Oval Office and across the South Lawn to Marine One.

He stopped in front of the marine who was standing guard by the helicopter and gave the most respectful salute. Donald Trump had been in many helicopters—and private planes, for that matter—but that look of reverence in his eyes told me this time was different.

For the August trip to Bedminster, we needed to be as persuasive as ever in order to get him to agree to it. He didn't want to go for long, certainly not ten days. In the summer of 2017, when the West Wing underwent a much-needed renovation, he had gone to his club for two weeks and been destroyed by the media. They had suggested he was merely taking a vacation, and nothing could have been further from the truth. I'm not even sure the word *vacation* is in Donald Trump's vocabulary.

Besides, every president gets out of Washington in August for a week or longer. The city all but shuts down. Congress is out of session, and the weather is just miserable. President Barack

Obama used to go to Martha's Vineyard, while George W. Bush took off for his ranch in Crawford, Texas.

When President Trump returned from those two weeks in 2017, he told us, "I'm never going away for that long again."

He wasn't kidding. Even when he went on foreign trips, he wanted the schedule to be as condensed as possible. Often he would leave late so he could fly through the night and land in the morning in time for him to start his workday. It was grueling for the staff, but the president didn't want to be gone one moment longer than necessary.

"I will sleep on the plane," he used to say.

This time, we felt he had no choice.

"Sir, you have to go to Bedminster," we told him. "They're working on the air-conditioning system in the Oval and updating a couple of things in the residence, so you physically will not be able to work or live in the White House. Mrs. Trump will be in Bedminster. Barron [their thirteen-year-old son] will be there, and so will Ivanka, Jared [Kushner, Ivanka's husband], and their kids. We will make sure it's a productive week, that you will do as much or as little as you want. It will go by very quickly, we promise you."

Mission accomplished.

Of course, once we got him to Bedminster, there was no guarantee that he would want to stay there. It wouldn't have surprised any of us if, halfway through the ten days, he had told us, "I'm wasting my time here, and I'm getting killed by the press. Why can't we leave for DC tomorrow so I can get back to work?"

It never got to that point, thank goodness, and that was because he kept busy, catching up on calls and paperwork, while also receiving briefings from his advisors.

He also took advantage of some sorely needed time off. I worked with the club's golf pro to set up foursomes for the president with friends, members of Congress, and prominent businessmen. He prefers to play with golfers at his level or better.

One night, the president enjoyed a family dinner, and on the Friday before we left, he dined with Mrs. Trump and Tim Cook, the CEO of Apple. The three had a wonderful time.

By the eve of our return to the capital, slated for Sunday morning, August 18, he seemed as content as ever and more confident, too. I'm not suggesting that he wasn't in complete control from the start. It was just that like others who had occupied that office before him, with each day that went by, each crisis he faced, for better or worse, he grew more and more into the role.

For me, it was an honor to watch up close as he further grasped the subtleties of such a formidable challenge. As he relaxed, the staff could relax. As with any job, we felt secure only when the boss was pleased.

★

Much to be proud of happened in those ten days. Take the events we held in Pennsylvania and New Hampshire.

Unless you are in the arena and observe how excited people get to see Donald Trump in person, you can't possibly appreciate what a rock star he is. Television gives you a glimpse of that, but it does not come close to capturing the remarkable atmosphere. I've never been to a rock concert with more energy than a Trump rally.

His supporters routinely show up at the arena the night before; many stand for hours and hours, waiting for their hero to arrive. I normally watched the speech from the staff viewing

area, close to the stage, and never failed to recognize how fortunate I was.

Such a rally is most likely the only time these people will
ever see the president up close. I saw him up close, day after day,
for more than two and a half years.

At the podium for about ninety minutes, he isn't a phony,
like countless others in public office. He relates to everybody
in the building as if they were lifelong friends. He does not talk
*at* them; he talks *to* them, much as President Franklin Delano
Roosevelt did during those famous fireside chats on the radio in
the 1930s and '40s.

It's precisely what many people are yearning for, as they
struggle to get by in a country that seems to have forgotten they
exist. The president doesn't forget, not for a second. He makes
them feel that they matter, and to know there is somebody in
the White House fighting for them raises their spirits like nothing else. Other politicians have let them down, over and over.
Sure, they said all the right things about increasing our wages,
protecting our borders, improving our health care, and so on.
But, in the end, those politicians have had more in common
with one another than with the citizens they are supposed to
serve. That goes for Republicans as well as Democrats.

Without question, no one gets more out of the rallies than
President Donald J. Trump. No wonder he feels so energized
whenever he is on the road. He is reminded of all the good work
he is doing for this country that the press never bothers to report
on, and for which the Democrats never give him credit.

Take prison reform, something the Democrats have been
talking about forever. The president got behind the issue, leading to shorter sentences and job training for prisoners, and only

a handful of Democrats praised him for the vital role he played. I'm not implying he did it to receive the credit, although it sure would be nice.

When he's speaking at those rallies and sees how the people react to him, he remembers: *This* is why I'm the president. For these people right here.

People tend to forget how much of the country voted for him. Every so often, when he hosted CEOs whose companies focused on issues that affected mostly rural areas or members of Congress from Middle America, he would call out from the Oval Office, "Madeleine, bring in the map."

The map broke down, state by state, county by county, who had voted for him and who had voted for Hillary Clinton. The East and West Coasts were mostly blue. The rest of the country was filled with red.

Like Vanna White in *Wheel of Fortune*, I would walk into the Oval Office proudly holding the map.

"Look at all that red," he'd say.

At times the staff grew discouraged by the barrage of attacks from the media and also needed to be reminded of who we served. It's easy to lose sight of that while sipping a cocktail in a swanky DC hotel. Like it or not, we're also part of the elite.

The people at the Trump rallies do not care about what the *New York Times* or the *Washington Post* says they should care about: the Russia investigation, the president's income taxes— you name it. They care about feeding their families, paying their bills, and keeping their country safe.

As for the events we held in August, they were like many other events during the 2016 campaign and ever since, Donald Trump being . . . Donald Trump.

In Pennsylvania, at a petrochemical complex still under construction about thirty miles from Pittsburgh, he touched on so many topics that it was hard to keep track: the Paris Agreement on climate change, the Green New Deal, immigration, Iran, China—even the Academy Awards, which had been held way back in February.

No one, the president said, watches the Oscars anymore because of the celebrities "disrespecting the people in this room."

Amen.

Two days later, at the rally in Manchester, New Hampshire, he went off against "radical socialism" and brought up one of its chief advocates, Massachusetts senator Elizabeth Warren.

Once Donald Trump gets rolling, it's impossible to stop him, and why would you even bother? 2020, here we come!

The rest of the August trip was just as productive, starting with two fund-raisers in the Hamptons. The first was held at the home of the real estate developer Stephen Ross, who is 95 percent owner of the Miami Dolphins football team; the second at a 17,000-square-foot mansion belonging to another billionaire developer and Republican donor.

The program was the same for both. The president began in a photo line with guests and then conducted a roundtable with twenty or so of the major donors. It was supposed to go for roughly twenty minutes. As usual, it didn't. The man likes to talk. Which is totally fine. He is the president of the United States. He can talk as long as he wants. Each donor contributed $100,000, perhaps more. They deserved their money's worth.

Speaking of the upcoming election, we also had a political meeting at Bedminster. We held one every month or so to get an update on how we stood in each state. So far, so good, no matter what the polls were saying about this Democrat or that Democrat claiming the advantage in a potential one-on-one showdown. Remember, the pollsters in 2016 said that Hillary Clinton would be the next president.

In earlier discussions, the president had told us he would drop by this particular meeting for only a couple of minutes. He ended up staying for three hours.

That shocked no one, and as usual, he didn't just sit there and listen; he posed one probing question after another. It's remarkable how involved he gets on intricate political matters.

"How many staff members do we have in this state?"

"How much money have we raised here?"

"Should we put more resources in this part of the country?"

The media have constantly speculated on who the president and his team were hoping to run against. Truth was, he wavered. One week, he would say, "Please let it be Bernie [Sanders]. I would love to go against him in a debate." Another week, he would be praying to take on former vice president Joe Biden or Senator Warren.

Whoever it would turn out to be, the feeling in the West Wing was the same: we got this.

★

Sitting by the pool that afternoon, I felt vindicated for having pushed as hard as I had to make it to Bedminster in the first place.

There were some on the White House staff who didn't feel I should be there. As a matter of fact, they were never in favor of my traveling with the president. Some of them had worked their entire careers to acquire such access, and now, out of nowhere, came a twenty-six-year-old assistant with no experience in government—and she gets to spend as much time with the president as we do? We can't allow that to happen.

Those staff members didn't say it in so many words, but I'm certain the fact that I am a woman made them resent me even further. The people who tried over and over to hold me back— and I am not just talking about going on trips—were men. That can't be a coincidence.

Most threatening to them was how close the president and I seemed to be. He trusted me, and there aren't many people he trusts. His wife. His family. His closest friends. Maybe a handful of others, such as Hope Hicks, who was then director of strategic communications, and Dan Scavino, who was director of social media, but that's about it.

Over time I became privy to information about Donald Trump and his family that other staffers were not. I never planned it that way, it just happened. I think—and I hope I'm not being presumptuous—that the president saw me almost as another daughter. I definitely saw him as a father figure. He was very kind and thoughtful and took care of me, just like my own dad.

"Where's Madeleine?" the president asked several times when he was on Air Force One or Marine One. "Why isn't she with us?"

Access, it may come as no surprise, meant everything in the Trump White House, and I'm sure it was not much different in previous administrations. The closer you were to the president physically, and the more time you spent with him, the more important you were—or were perceived to be. That explains why many staffers complained on a regular basis if they weren't in the spot they thought matched their position.

On occasion, I'm ashamed to admit, that included me. If somebody with significantly less status, perhaps a junior staffer from the the Eisenhower Executive Office Building (EEOB) sat in the same area as I did on Air Force One, I would feel frustrated.

Of course, when a woman complained, it wasn't treated with the same urgency as when a man did. The women who work in the White House, the members of this particular boys' club believe, should be grateful for anything they can get.

"Why are you making a big deal out of this?" a male staffer asked me on more than one occasion. "You're on the trip, aren't you? You're on Air Force One!" He never would have said that to a man.

Thank goodness there was one person who saw absolutely nothing wrong with a young woman gaining influence: Donald Trump. Goes against everything you've heard about him, doesn't it?

It happens to be true. The president respects women more than any other man I have worked for. Hope Hicks. Kellyanne Conway. Sarah Sanders. Stephanie Grisham. Nikki Haley. Elaine Chao. The list goes on and on. And on a more personal level, needless to say, the first lady and Ivanka. Each woman is powerful and talented.

★

One night at Bedminster, I called the president to run something by him, and he mentioned that he and the first lady, having a movie night, had just been talking about me. The film was *Breakfast at Tiffany's*, one of my favorites.

"Melania said you remind her of Audrey Hepburn," the president said.

The iconic film, which was released in the fall of 1961 and based on a novel by Truman Capote, starred Hepburn and George Peppard.

"Honey," the president joked with her, "that might very well be the nicest compliment you've ever given."

I was in such good spirits that when Hogan Gidley, the White House principal deputy press secretary, who had mentioned the dinner earlier, asked me again if I wanted to join him and the reporters, I surprised myself. I said, "Sure, why not?"

It was Saturday night, and I had nothing else to do. I had given some thought to attending a bachelorette party for a friend in Montauk, a village on Long Island, but decided that it was too far away and I wouldn't get back in time to leave with everyone for DC the next morning.

The fact that I had been drinking throughout the day and my defenses were down also had something to do with my changing my mind. I never would have agreed to a dinner with reporters if I had been completely sober.

No doubt I shouldn't have been drinking in the first place. Especially after what I knew about the damage alcohol can cause.

I had two upsetting experiences in my past that were due to excessive drinking.

At a party in high school, I kissed a guy whose girlfriend was in another room. Someone saw us, and everyone at the party found out. The girlfriend and her friends held it against me for the rest of high school even though the guy had been the one to initiate it. What made it worse was that it was my first kiss and will always be my first kiss.

You think that's embarrassing? That was nothing compared to what happened in college. I was kicked out of my

sorority, Alpha Delta Pi, for drinking when I was an intern at
our national headquarters in Atlanta, Georgia. I can't pretend
that I didn't know the rules. I was the president of my chapter
at the College of Charleston. I knew all the rules. Nevertheless,
just like that, something dear to me was taken away for good.

Yet there I was with a few drinks in my system, agreeing to
spend time with people who were, essentially, strangers. Dinner,
without question, would include more alcohol.

Those types of get-togethers are actually fairly common on
the road. The press sees such a dinner as a chance to get better acquainted with members of the White House staff, and to
ensure that it's a social and not official occasion, it's made clear
at the outset that everything is off the record.

Hogan and I left for dinner around seven. I was nervous.
I wasn't sure if the reporters would approve of me. What if I
bored them? What if they didn't like me? It was too late, though,
to back out now.

Besides, I felt comfortable around Hogan, who, although
about ten years older, was one of my better friends in the West
Wing. He was superb at promoting the president and his agenda
but also kind and sensitive. I knew he would have my back.
What could go wrong?

After a roughly twenty-minute drive, we arrived at the
Embassy Suites, where most of the media were staying, and
met our companions for the evening: Philip Rucker of the
*Washington Post*, Andrew Restuccia of the *Wall Street Journal*,
Jennifer Jacobs of Bloomberg, and Steve Holland of Reuters.

When Hogan and I walked in, I thanked the reporters for
allowing me to join them. We then made our way to the Liberty
Grille, the hotel restaurant.

The only person I knew even vaguely was Steve, who I thought was a fair reporter and who had always been warm toward me. I had been Steve's guest a few months before at the Gridiron Club dinner in DC, which has long been one of the most important gatherings of the year. The others I recognized from the daily press pools. The most I had ever said to them was something like "The president is ready for you." Engaging with the media any further than that was out of the question.

The Liberty Grille wasn't fancy. We took a rounded booth toward the back of the room. I sat at the end.

The six of us hadn't been seated for more than a few minutes when the reporters suggested we order some wine and asked whether I liked white or red. I said I preferred white but would be fine with whatever they wanted. We ordered one bottle of white and one bottle of red, and the drinks kept flowing.

Soon afterward, Hogan left to do a live hit on Judge Jeanine Pirro's show on Fox, which he could do from the hotel. He had told me about the interview earlier, so I'd known that he would be leaving. I figured he would be gone for twenty minutes at the most. I should have known better. Judge Jeanine, who is incredibly passionate in her support for the president, has a good rapport with Hogan and sometimes keeps him on air for longer than scheduled.

He wound up being gone for more than an hour.

I should have been more nervous without him there. I wasn't. Quite the opposite; I felt comfortable, and I thought I was in total control. For a change, I was the center of attention, not Hogan, and as much as I thought of myself as someone who preferred to be out of the spotlight, a part of me relished it. It comes from a need for approval and a desire to please others, which goes back as long as I can remember and may have something to do with my parents divorcing when I was only four years old. I always wanted to be the perfect daughter, the perfect student, the perfect everything.

I don't remember how many glasses of Sauvignon Blanc I drank, but it did its job. It didn't make matters better that I had had those drinks by the pool and hadn't eaten anything since breakfast.

Everyone thought that Hogan would be back soon, so we waited to order dinner. We waited, and waited—and kept drinking. Meanwhile, the reporters started to ask questions, one after another. They had me, the president's executive assistant, all to themselves. Better yet, they had somebody they knew never spoke to the press. North Korea, Iran, the border controversy, the tax bill; they did not ask anything about those issues. They had plenty of sources for policy matters.

No, they were looking for something juicy concerning the president and the lives of the first family, the kind of palace intrigue they couldn't find anywhere else.

"How do you think Barron is adjusting to living in the White House?"

"What is the president's relationship with Tiffany like?"

I gave them answers with great enthusiasm, reveling in the most unusual role for me. I know that to be the truth, even if I can't recall everything I said.

"Barron is a typical thirteen-year-old boy. Sometimes I think he'd rather be playing video games than walking from the residence to Marine One with tons of cameras on him."

"Tiffany is a young woman trying to find her way," is my best recollection of what I essentially said. "That's hard to do when you're the president's daughter. I know she's glad to be in DC, close to her dad."

Hogan must have been shocked when he returned to see me holding court. That couldn't have been what he had anticipated. I had hardly ever said two words to a reporter, and now I was leading the conversation. He sat down to order dinner—the rest of us had finally eaten—and we stayed for a while longer.

Believe me, I had no intention of going to that dinner to dish on the first family. I cared about them very much, but I said some things I never should have said.

To anyone anywhere and most of all, not to a group of reporters.

Because I did, my life will never be the same.

# CHAPTER TWO

# *Signs of Trouble*

After dinner, I shared an Uber with some of my dinner companions back to my hotel, where they were also staying. Hogan, who was going back to Bedminster, didn't object, even if it meant more time for me to be alone with them, more time to talk. Once I arrived at the hotel, though, I went right to bed. It was quite late, and I had definitely drunk too much.

The first sign of trouble arrived the next morning, waiting for me when I woke up. It was a text from Jennifer Jacobs:

> you are *so much fun* to hang out with. thanks for
> joining us for that off the record dinner.

I could definitely let my guard down when I was with my friends, but finding out I was "so much fun to hang out with" was something I was surprised to hear from a reporter. It had not been a social dinner, no matter how casual the others had tried to make it. In work settings, I was usually pretty serious. I was focused on my work.

It would have made more sense for Jennifer to write something such as "Thanks, Madeleine, for coming to dinner with us. It was so great to get to know you. I hope we can do it again soon."

I couldn't help but wonder: What did I say that was so entertaining?

Oh, well, maybe I was just overreacting after another taxing week. Regardless of how successful the trip had been, it was still an enormous undertaking. That's always the case when the president goes on the road.

Calls must still be made and appointments arranged. If anything, it's harder to keep everything together. When I was in the Outer Oval Office, the area outside the Oval Office, the president was in my line of sight, but when we traveled, I was forced to rely on others to pass along messages or receive any instructions. That didn't always go smoothly.

One afternoon earlier that week, I had been in the pro shop, when, by coincidence, I was told that the president was looking for me. I got into a golf cart and found him as he was about to tee off on one of the holes. He was playing with an old friend and wanted to tell me to make sure to schedule a visit to the White House for him. As I said before, the man never stops working. I can't tell you how many times I would later hear how, during a round of golf, he added events or meetings to his schedule.

That's why I couldn't let my guard down, even for a second. Not until I sat by the pool on Saturday morning did I feel I could finally relax.

Or maybe I wasn't overreacting.

Two hours after reading Jennifer's text, I was sitting with other junior staff members in the waiting area at Morristown Municipal Airport in New Jersey, for the flight back to DC. The president had yet to arrive on Marine One. The staff who weren't manifested on Marine One, along with the press corps, always traveled to the airport in advance of the president. While we waited, I suddenly got the feeling that every member of the press corps was staring at me.

They had never paid much attention to me. I didn't think I was very important to them.

The wheels in my head continued to spin: *Please get me on this plane as fast as humanly possible. I don't want to spend another second trapped in this room with these people. . . . Please!*

My wish was granted. We were finally aboard Air Force One, and those paranoid thoughts went away. I sat near Hogan and the other traveling staff. No one mentioned the dinner. Surely, if he had been concerned, Hogan would have said something to me.

It's impossible not to feel on top of the world when you are riding in an airplane with the president of the United States, flown by air force pilots and protected by the Secret Service. There is no place I have ever felt more secure. Even turbulence can't contend with Air Force One. It's amazing!

When I got back to DC, I told Ben, my boyfriend, about the events in Pennsylvania and New Hampshire and about how the president had asked me to fly with him on Marine One after an event. I can't tell you how big a thrill that was, bigger even than Air Force One. Just six or seven people, in addition to the Secret

Service, can be on board at any time. More often than not, the spots are reserved for the senior staff or the president's family.

Too bad the ride doesn't last long, sometimes as little as ten minutes. I always wished it would go on forever, and I can say that about a lot of things connected to this dream job. I tried to be nonchalant, as if I rode on Marine One every day. It was impossible.

I flew on the helicopter only a handful of times, and it was always a tremendous honor. I would be sitting directly across from the president, trying to take in the gorgeous views he kept pointing out, while also attending to any requests he might have.

I didn't tell Ben about the dinner with the reporters. It didn't seem important at the time, or maybe I just didn't want to relive it with him.

As a matter of fact, I didn't give the dinner a moment's thought—until I got an email the following Tuesday morning from Stephanie Grisham, the White House press secretary. Stephanie wanted to see me in her office the moment I came in.

All of a sudden, that dinner became the only thing I could think about. Why else would Stephanie summon me first thing in the morning? She never asked to see me privately in her office. Whatever she might want, it must be serious, and I could think of nothing else I had done at Bedminster or anywhere else that had anything to do with the press.

I dropped my purse onto my desk and went to her office. I didn't even turn on my computer or chat with anybody in the Outer Oval Office. I wanted to get it over with as fast as possible.

As soon as I got there, Stephanie closed the door, another bad sign. My stomach started to churn, and I could feel my face becoming red and burning up, which happens whenever I get anxious.

It wasn't that I was worried about being fired, although I was fully aware of how fast things can change in the Trump White House, and it didn't take long to learn that lesson.

In February 2017, three weeks after President Trump was sworn in, Michael Flynn, his national security advisor, was forced to resign. He had been accused of lying to the vice president about conversations he had held with Russian officials in 2016. It was a huge story. I didn't know him very well, but I knew he'd been a trusted and loyal advisor on the campaign and during the transition. If someone that senior could be ousted, no one was safe.

It hit much closer to home about a year later when I got a call from someone in General John Kelly's office. The general was the White House chief of staff at the time.

"Can you send John down?" General Kelly's assistant asked, referring to John McEntee, President Trump's body man, probably my best friend in the West Wing.

The body man—and a lot of politicians have one—is the individual who travels with the principal and carries a variety of objects he or she might require at any moment. For Donald Trump, that usually meant his Tic Tacs, mouthwash, Sharpies, hair spray, and challenge coins.

"John went out to grab lunch," I said. "I'll let you know as soon he gets back."

That wasn't good enough.

"Can you tell him he needs to get back here right away?" the assistant went on. "He needs to meet with the White House counsel's office."

I tracked John down, and he hurried back. Less than an hour later, someone from Human Resources came into our office to grab his coat and other personal items. I had to point out which items belonged to him and which were the property of the White House.

"Where's John?" I asked.

"He's not coming back," the HR woman said. She said nothing else.

I was shocked and very hurt. It was not merely the fact they had gotten rid of him; it was the way they had done so, with no explanation or compassion for how he might feel. He wouldn't find out the reason for months.

John, as it turned out, had a gambling problem. I understood why General Kelly felt he had to let him go, though I didn't agree with him then and still don't. Furthermore, John was as devoted to protecting the president as the Secret Service agents were. He would have taken a bullet for him.

I suppose I shouldn't have been so shocked. From your first day on the job, it's drilled into you that as a political appointee, you serve "at the pleasure of the president." I have no problem with that. He's the president; he should be able to fire whomever he wants whenever he wants.

Like a lot of my colleagues, getting fired was always in the back of my mind. I contend that if you work in the West Wing and that thought does *not* occur to you from time to time, there's something wrong with you.

The best way for many of us to cope with the fear was to make light of it.

"Maybe they won't let me back in," I used to tell the others in the Outer Oval whenever I left town for more than a day or two. It was common among the staff to joke that the way we would find out we'd been let go was when our badges wouldn't work at the gate.

Not everyone thought it was funny.

★

Stephanie didn't waste time with small talk. With her dark hair and piercing blue eyes, she was as intimidating as anybody else in the building. I thought of her as a friend, but she took her job very seriously, and that would obviously come first.

"I heard about the dinner," she said.

She went on to tell me what she had been told I had said at the dinner. That the president's twenty-six-year-old daughter, Tiffany, was having difficulties with her weight and that Barron kept pretty much to himself.

Stephanie, having worked for the first lady as her deputy chief of staff and communications director, was particularly concerned about what I might have said about Mrs. Trump's only child. I would have felt the same way.

I didn't deny a word of it. How could I? I had been drinking. I couldn't remember everything I'd said to the reporters.

There was no need to panic, though. Stephanie said she'd been given the heads-up from another journalist, who was "friendly to us" but hadn't been at the dinner. Not every reporter in Washington wanted to see us fail.

Whether that meant friendly to the administration or to Stephanie, I didn't bother to ask. Nor did I ask for the identity of the reporter. If she had wanted me to know, she would have told me.

She then offered a little advice. "I want to remind you that nothing is ever off the record," she said. "Be really careful about what you say."

"Should I do anything at this point?" I asked.

"Like what, tell the president?"

"No, no, not that, but should I email the reporters and remind them that the dinner was off the record?"

"Madeleine, if you want to email them, go ahead. I can't imagine that it would hurt."

I did just that as soon I got back to my desk. The only one of the four I didn't reach out to was Jennifer Jacobs, who had confirmed in her text on Sunday that the dinner had indeed been off the record. I took my time drafting the email. It had to be just right.

The email to the other three reporters went something like this: "Thank you so much for including me in that off-the-record dinner on Saturday night. I had a really wonderful time."

The three weren't fooled for an instant. They knew my sole purpose was to put the words "off the record" in writing and make sure they didn't raise any objections. I didn't send the emails to compile a paper trail but rather for my own peace of mind. I couldn't be sure of anything anymore.

The reporters got back to me right away, and, boy, did I feel like an idiot. They each replied how much they had enjoyed the dinner and that, yes, the conversation had been private.

I thought, for a moment, of responding "I did not mean to insinuate that you were going to share anything I said," but decided against it. The best thing for me to do now was to let the matter drop and get back to work.

I was so relieved that I didn't bother to tell Stephanie how they had responded. She had enough to deal with. It occurred to me that I had probably been freaking out for no reason.

Again, the dinner was out of my mind, and everything went back to normal, at least as normal as life can ever be at 1600 Pennsylvania Avenue.

Until Thursday morning, when Hogan called me into his office.

Hogan, like Stephanie, never called me into his office. He might ask me to stop by when we ran into each other by the Oval Office, but this was different. This was another summons. My face began to burn and my stomach churned, when he, too, closed the door.

For more than two and a half years, I had walked around the building in complete control, going wherever I wanted, seeing whomever I wanted at any time. Now, for the second time in three days, I felt as though I had no control at all, and it terrified me.

He, like Stephanie, got right to the point. Two of the four reporters from the dinner, he told me, had warned him that the other two were sharing what I had said with their colleagues. The two who warned Hogan were Jennifer Jacobs and Steve Holland. That didn't surprise me, knowing Steve as I did, and I could tell that Jennifer, as the only other woman at the dinner, might be more empathetic.

Besides, from what I had been told and from the slanted way they covered the Trump White House, Phil Rucker and Andrew Restuccia were seen as troublemakers. The president referred to Rucker's newspaper as "the Amazon *Washington Post*" in reference to its owner, Jeff Bezos, the founder of Amazon. It wasn't a compliment.

Anyway, I couldn't believe this was happening. Every time I thought the stupid dinner was behind me, someone else brought it up.

Yet again, there was no reason to panic. According to Hogan, Steve and Jennifer had also said that they had reminded their two colleagues the dinner was off the record and they shouldn't be sharing the details with anyone else.

Everything will be fine, Hogan assured me. I told him I would like to thank Jennifer and Steve. They had my back, and I appreciated that more than you can imagine. That doesn't happen very often in the cesspool that is the nation's capital. Most people care only about protecting themselves and their precious careers.

I don't want you to do that, Hogan told me firmly. They had come to him as a courtesy and he was sure they didn't want anyone else to know. We should keep it that way.

Absolutely, I said.

I did ask Hogan, as I had asked Stephanie, if there was anything I could do to make the problem go away. No, he said. Just go back to your desk and do your job.

That I could do.

As usual, there were tons of calls to place for the president and tons of requests for his time. I realized how silly of me it had been to worry about an off-the-record dinner at a restaurant somewhere in New Jersey when there were countless other pressing matters to focus on.

Besides, on Saturday morning, I would be flying home to California to undergo a minor operation to remove a bump on the bridge of my nose that had been bothering me since, I swear, I was fifteen. I was so self-conscious about it that in high school, I had refused to sit in front of any boy I thought was cute. I was terrified of turning to the side and his catching a glimpse of my unattractive profile.

I told barely anyone about the operation. It was so minor that most of my close friends, and even my family, didn't notice anything different afterward. For so long, it had been the *only* thing I had noticed when I looked in the mirror, so to me it made all the difference in the world.

Throughout the day on Friday, I kept looking for the right time to let the president know I would be gone for the week, but something always got in the way. I hadn't told him earlier because there was no reason to bother him with my vacation plans until the last minute. I wasn't looking forward to it. He doesn't like it when the people he relies on are gone for longer than a day.

Finally, around seven, I got the chance. He was walking out the door that opened onto the West Wing colonnade, known as "the president's walk," which leads to the main structure of the White House. He was on his way to the elevator that would take him to the private residence. Vice President Pence was with him.

"Mr. President," I said, "I just want to tell you that I'm having minor surgery next week and Molly will take over." Molly Michael had joined us in the Outer Oval in August 2018.

"You're leaving," the president said, sounding surprised and, I dare say, a bit upset.

"I will be gone for about a week," I told him.

Or so I thought.

The next morning, I boarded the flight to San Diego. I couldn't have been more relieved to get out of Washington. I loved that job, don't get me wrong, but I also loved having a personal life, and you don't get to have much of one when you work at the White House—that is, if you want to keep working there.

Everyone else in the West Wing had taken a break that summer. I had volunteered to go to Bedminster so my three Outer Oval Office colleagues, Dan Scavino, Nick Luna, and Molly, could take their vacations. Now it was my turn.

It was safe to say that I wouldn't be able to stay off the grid entirely. Frankly, I always became more anxious whenever I was out of the building for a few days. I would check my email every half hour or so, wondering: Is the president done yet with this morning's intelligence briefing? Who will keep him on schedule? Is he getting enough downtime?

I was worrying for no reason.

"Molly did such a fantastic job," the president had once told me after I had gotten back from a previous trip.

"Sir, that is really wonderful," I'd said, but it had just made me nervous for my own job security. I had told myself, and I was only half kidding: I'm never going on vacation again!

Everybody in that building always had a sense that if you were gone for any significant period of time, you would miss out or something would happen that, you believe, you might have been able to prevent. I noticed that on several occasions with

Jared and Ivanka, who both worked in the West Wing. They would go on a vacation or working trip, and all of a sudden, a meeting would be put onto the calendar that ran counter to a policy that one or both was promoting.

So during the first few days in California, even as I was recovering from the surgery at my mom's house in La Jolla, I checked in with Molly from time to time. She was quite competent, as the president had noted, but the two didn't connect the way he and I did. Molly was more reserved. I would often have to encourage her to speak up when the president asked for something from the Oval Office.

"Do you see any potential problems this week?" I asked. "Do you need any numbers?" In my contacts, I had every phone number the president might possibly require.

"Thanks, Madeleine, I'm good," Molly said. "We will see you when you get back. Enjoy your time off."

I promised I would do just that. I even got over my initial regret that the president was in the Oval Office that week. Originally, the plan had been for him to take a trip to Europe, which was why I had scheduled surgery for the last week of August. I'd never have dreamed of being out of the office for an extended period of time when he was at the White House.

If he was in the Oval, *I* was at my desk.

Unfortunately, the trip was canceled, and by then, it was too late. If I didn't keep that appointment, I wasn't sure when I'd have another chance to go through with the surgery.

Besides, once we got past Labor Day, which was a week from then, I probably wouldn't be allowed another extended break until after the 2020 election. That was a long fifteen months away. The campaign would soon be in full swing, the first contest, in Iowa, set for the first week of February. All hands on deck!

Securing the nomination obviously wasn't the issue, but it's never too early to begin planning for the general election. The Democrats, whomever they were to put up, would be motivated as never before, the press fully in their pocket.

Since early that summer, I had sat in on the weekly Monday-morning political meetings, which did not include the president. I had asked for more responsibility in my role, and I had gotten it. Jared suggested, "Let's get you more involved with the campaign."

The president also mentioned that I would be going on the campaign trail with him. I was thrilled beyond belief. More rallies. More fund-raisers. More time with him on Air Force One and maybe even Marine One. As awesome as that dream job was, the best was yet to come.

Ever since White House press secretary Sarah Sanders, who had accomplished so much at a young age, had left in June, I had begun to envision how I could serve as more than an executive assistant. Perhaps, in a second Trump administration, I thought, I could serve as the deputy chief of staff.

Why not? It had happened before. During President Obama's second term, Anita Decker Breckenridge had been promoted from personal secretary to deputy chief of staff for operations.

In the meantime, I planned to enjoy every minute of my week at home in southern California. I would watch movies, catch up on shows, and walk my dog, Lucy, a terrier mutt, every evening to the ocean to watch the sunset. Lucy is eleven years old, but whenever she gets to a beach, she runs around like a puppy. In a way, I felt the same: free.

The fresh ocean air was exactly what I needed. Washington in late August is unbearably hot and muggy. The White House could wait.

## CHAPTER THREE

# Serving at the Pleasure of the President

The call came on Thursday, around 3:00 p.m. California time, from Mick Mulvaney, the president's acting chief of staff. He didn't leave a message, which I thought was rather odd.

I had been taking a nap. I was resting a lot, recovering from the surgery. As each day passed, I felt more relaxed, able to leave the pressures of DC behind.

I texted him as soon as I saw the missed call:

Is everything okay?

I figured he must have a question related to the day's schedule or another matter that only I could answer. There hadn't been time to tell Molly everything before I had taken off for San Diego. No worries; I was sure I'd be able to give him whatever he needed.

"I was just calling to check in," he immediately texted back.

Now I was really confused. Why would Mick want to just "check in"? He and I got along well enough, but he wasn't a check-in kind of guy with me, and as chaotic as life can get in the West Wing, there appeared no reason to reach out while I was on vacation, unless it was something really urgent. I called him.

"This is going to be a very difficult conversation," he said.

I knew right away what he was referring to, and unlike in the chats with Stephanie and Hogan, he wasn't interested in giving me a warning. It was too late for that.

"I found out about the dinner, and I had to tell the president about it," he said. "He has been thinking about it all day, and we have decided you can't come back to the Oval Office. We're going to have to ask you to resign."

"Okay, I understand," I said, not missing a beat.

Somehow I was able to remain calm, even as I felt my world come crashing down. I must have been in shock.

I can't remember anything else I might have said to Mick. It couldn't have been much. The conversation was over before I knew it.

Why didn't I push back? you may wonder. After all, I loved my job more than anything. So wouldn't I have done just about anything to keep it?

Besides, I had been working for President Trump for more than two and a half years, starting well before Mick had come to the West Wing in January 2019. Hadn't I earned the right to speak to the president himself, not an intermediary? Let's be honest: Mick was the chief of staff in name only. The president never took away "acting" from his title.

Maybe I should have pushed back, but knowing the president as well as I did, I wasn't surprised I had heard it from Mick. For somebody who built a brand on the line "You're fired!," Donald Trump, contrary to what many people assume, doesn't actually enjoy firing people. He delegates that unpleasant chore to someone else, often his chief of staff.

I didn't push back for two reasons.

One, I was in no position, due to the alcohol, to deny anything that was alleged, and even if I did, it would be my word against the word of four respected journalists, a fight I would lose every time. I had done something wrong, that was clear, and the only noble thing at that point was to accept the consequences. That's how I was brought up.

Second, remember, I served "at the pleasure of the president," which was, apparently, no longer the case. Who was I, an executive assistant, to challenge that?

No sooner did I put the phone down than my mom walked in. She had heard the sound of my voice from the other room. She could tell it wasn't a routine phone call. Moms always know.

I told her what Mick had said and went on to tell her about the dinner. Until then, I hadn't told a soul. Seriously, before Mick reached out, what could I possibly have said? "Hey, Mom, listen, I went to this dinner last week with reporters, and I got really drunk and said something I shouldn't have said about President Trump's kids. Just thought you should know . . . can you pass the butter?"

I had been ashamed of myself and wanted more than anything to pretend it had never happened. If it were to blow over, as I prayed it would, there'd be no reason to ever tell her—or anyone.

Mom and I hugged. She was devastated for me, knowing how I felt about my job and the president, and worried, with good reason, that I would beat myself up over it.

In any case, I didn't have to remain calm anymore. I could cry in her arms as long, and as hysterically, as necessary.

Except there was little time for that. Not now. There were too many matters that needed to get resolved, and quickly. When is the resignation effective? Am I required to submit a formal letter? What will happen to all of my personal belongings in my desk? Who else in the building knows I'm leaving? Those were just for starters.

To get some answers, I called Emma Doyle, the principal deputy chief of staff. She could not have been more compassionate, and I will always be grateful for that. I needed to hear a friendly voice as never before. Sometimes that is all you need.

Emma wasn't certain if I had to write a letter—I never did—but the resignation would be effective immediately, though, as it would turn out, I would continue to be paid through the end of September. That was a relief. People later told me I should have asked for a longer severance. I disagree. It was important for me to leave the West Wing, and the president, without causing any more trouble.

I then asked Emma the most vital question of all: Will the White House keep this quiet?

"Absolutely," she assured me. "We certainly don't want the cause for your resignation to ever get out."

I believed her. Every time somebody left the administration, and it happened fairly often, the press blew it out of proportion. That's what the press does, especially with this president.

Fortunately, by Emma's count, in addition to herself, only six others in the White House were aware of my situation: the president, Mick, Stephanie, Hogan, Dan Walsh, the deputy chief of staff for operations, and Pat Cipollone, the White House counsel. That wasn't an especially wide circle. There seemed to be every reason to think the story could be contained.

Furthermore, Emma said, they would try to help me find another position in the administration or outside the government if that is what I wanted. I had made a big mistake, but I had been extremely loyal to the president, his family, and the entire team from the moment I had started. That had to count for something.

After I hung up with Emma, I felt better. Yes, I was losing a job that I treasured, but I would survive. No one would ever know what had happened. If anyone were to ask, the White House would simply explain that I had decided to move on, and the media would forget about it. That happens in Washington all the time, in every administration.

Better but still heartbroken. In between phone calls—sometimes *during* phone calls—I did my fair share of crying that day and in the days ahead. Each time I told someone, I felt as though I were going through the whole nightmare all over again.

Talking about what had happened with my dad was just as difficult, but he told me how much he loved me and said that I would get through it. That helped a great deal.

Talking to the rest of my family, especially my three grandparents, was the worst. I had let them down. They had been so proud of me, sharing with everyone they knew the fact that their granddaughter worked in the White House. Not anymore.

I was fortunate to bring all of my grandparents to the White House while I worked there. My grandmother on my mom's side, whom I call Gammy, had even met the president when she came in for a tour around Easter in 2017. No question, it was one of the highlights of her life. Mom had been there, too. The president had taken one look at the three of us and said, "All of you look so much alike. I want you to know what a great job Madeleine is doing."

"We're praying for you!" Gammy responded. "You have a lot of support in Orange County, California."

She was in a daze as we walked out of the Oval Office. "I can't believe that just happened," she said.

Whenever I spoke to any of my grandparents over the phone, or in person, they asked one question after another.

"What's it like to see the president every day?"

"Is it as crazy there as it seems on the news?"

"How does it feel to fly on Air Force One?"

On and on they would go, but I told them very little. I knew better than to share details about the president, his family, or my job with anyone, including my family. I shared with them only what was public knowledge already.

That's what was so ironic about the entire ordeal. In a building filled with leakers, which annoyed me no end, I prided myself on keeping my mouth shut. The president, as a matter of fact, occasionally asked who I thought the leakers might be. I had my suspicions, but since I could never be sure, I always told him I didn't know.

Only now, as it turned out, I was the one with the biggest mouth of all. Equally frustrating was that I didn't believe a word of the negative things I was told I had said at the dinner, while those who spoke ill of the president and his family in private conversations have hung onto their jobs and in some cases been promoted.

Telling Ben was also incredibly painful. I waited until I knew he would be home from work. I would need his undivided attention.

It hit him harder than I thought. The future he had seen for us—he serves as a political appointee at the Pentagon—as successful professionals on a path to building a life together was now in real jeopardy. Which explains why, after he recovered from the initial shock, he focused on how to fix the mess as fast as possible. We were in it together.

Ben suggested I reach out to a former colleague of his, a media expert, who could help us develop a solid game plan for how to move on. It was not about how to get my job back; that possibility was gone. It was about how to keep my reputation intact in order to secure the next job.

Meanwhile, I was worried how my resignation would affect other members of my family. My cousin, for example, was beginning her freshman year of college. Having the same last name, which is unique, she was bound to be asked about me. Again I was filled with tremendous guilt.

One fear kept surfacing after another, some justified, others not. It became impossible to separate fact from fantasy. My mom saw what was happening and tried to get me to look for some inner tranquillity before I lost it entirely.

"Madeleine, please put your phone down," she pleaded. "You need to take a breath."

"I can't, Mom," I said. "I have so much to do, so many calls to make. I don't have a choice."

At least I was doing something. Which was a heck of a lot better than beating myself up. That would come later, and often.

I had two goals, depending on whom I contacted: first, to soften the blow for those I cared about who had yet to hear the news and, second, to get ahead of the story before it was too late. That was where the experience of working in the White House paid off big time. I was setting up my own one-person crisis communications center.

There was another reason I wouldn't listen to Mom: I was in denial. Working the phones, speaking to familiar voices, I was acting as if I were still in the West Wing.

Unfortunately, there was a cost. I started to feel that I was becoming a nuisance, people thinking "Why does she keep calling and asking for advice or giving us updates on what the press is saying? She doesn't work here anymore." Whenever I had called before, they had picked up the phone or called back right away, figuring it had something to do with the president. I realized for the first time that I no longer mattered, that they could choose not to call me back and there would be no consequences.

Before long, though, I noticed that I couldn't send any emails on my work phone. Wow, they don't waste any time, do they? When you're out, you are out! Still, to show how much I was in denial, I didn't think of myself at that moment. I thought only of the president and how he might be affected by my departure. When people email me, I wondered, once they don't get a response, how will they be able to reach him? Will the technicians in the White House forward my calls to Molly's phone? What will happen to the appointments he had been hoping to set up for weeks?

As usual, there was no end to what I worried about.

Then, around five, it arrived, the email that changed everything. It came from Maggie Haberman of the *New York Times*. No one in the press corps reveals the drama of the White House quite like Maggie does. She is the queen bee. Everyone talks to her, even if they deny it.

> Sorry to bother you—it's maggie Haberman at *NYT*. My colleague Annie Karni and I are preparing to report that you were dismissed from your job at EOP [Executive Office of the President] in relation to concerns by the president about indiscreet conversations with a group of reporters. I wanted to see if you wanted to comment. Thank you in advance for your time.

So much for keeping it quiet.

As I sat there reading her email over and over, the same crushing thoughts kept coming to me: My life is over. I will never get another job. I will be publicly humiliated. My reputation, and my family's reputation, will be ruined.

No, Maggie, I thought to myself, I do not want to comment. I want to crawl into a hole and never come out.

Over those next few minutes, I kept looking at my phone. I couldn't help myself. I had to see what Maggie and the other *Times* reporter would write about me, and soon enough, with my mom and younger sister, Katie, by my side, there it was on the internet, the headline making the situation more real and painful than ever: "Trump's Personal Assistant, Madeleine Westerhout, Steps Down."

I read the entire story, though I can't recall a word. Does it matter? The plain truth was there for everybody to see, and there wasn't a thing I could do about it.

Yet as horrible as I felt, I was, at least, grateful that there was nothing in the *Times* article, or anywhere else, about what I had supposedly said at the dinner in Bedminster. "Indiscreet" can refer to a lot of things.

I kept making calls over the next couple of hours until, mercifully, it became too late. I went to sleep, if you could call it that, checking my phone constantly, only there were no calls to make or emails to send. I couldn't remember the last time that had been the case. I was also still in a lot of discomfort from the splint the surgeon had put on my nose during the procedure on Monday, and I couldn't stop thinking about what might happen next.

I didn't have to wait long. On Friday morning, I received a text from Daniel Lippman, a reporter for Politico, the DC tabloid-like publication that's a must-read for everybody in government. I knew Daniel a bit, having spoken to him on background in connection with an article he had written about someone leaking the president's schedule. I had sent out a tweet, blasting the leaker, that had attracted a fair amount of attention.

His text to me was nasty, even by this town's low standards, and it wasn't solely because he listed the comments he was told I had supposedly made at the dinner. It was also because he included comments about me and my character, from anonymous sources, no less.

That I had a "ton of attitude." That I didn't have "a lot of friends." That, get this, I had been spotted at 5:30 or 6:00 p.m. on several occasions earlier that summer having a drink with my boyfriend at a private club close to the White House. Which wasn't true, for one thing. Besides, what that would have to do with me losing my job was beyond me.

"Do you have any comment on any of this?" he continued. "My deadline is ASAP."

I had thought that reading the email from Maggie Haberman was painful. Now I felt as if my heart was being ripped out.

Even so, the most prudent thing was to not say a word. That was the advice I had been given with regard to any media inquiries, of which there had been quite a few after the *Times* piece was posted.

It made perfect sense. I wasn't a press person. What if I were to say the wrong thing?

Only I didn't care about being prudent this time. Lippman's text was too revealing. I needed to respond.

Besides, as far as I could tell, no other journalist had uncovered such details. I thought—and it seems unbelievably naive in retrospect—that I might be able to keep him from filing his story.

I texted him back: "Could you please call me?"

When he did a few minutes later, I lost it, simple as that. Given what I had been going through since the call with Mick, which had been less than twenty-four hours earlier, it was bound to happen.

"You can write whatever you want to write about me," I told Lippman between tears, "but please leave the president's family out of this."

"I don't think I can do that," he said. "I'll talk to my editor."

I could tell from the sound of his voice that my plea would go nowhere. He had his scoop and was going to run with it, no matter who it might hurt. Perhaps that's how journalists have behaved forever in DC, I don't know, but that doesn't make it right.

The article went live a couple of hours later.

He wrote that I had been "fired after bragging to reporters that she had a better relationship with President Trump than his own daughters, Ivanka and Tiffany." Lippman also reported that I had said the "president did not like to be in pictures with Tiffany because he perceived her as overweight."

I was devastated yet again, and I wasn't sure how much more I could absorb. Reading the reference to Tiffany's weight really threw me off. It's the absolute worst thing one can ever say about another woman. I thought to myself, there's no way I could have said that.

Or was there?

In any case, I needed to remain strong, at least for the next several hours. There were two critical tasks I had to perform, and I couldn't afford to make any mistakes. I'd made enough already.

The first task was to craft a statement I would put out on Twitter. It would be my first, and probably only, opportunity to say something, in my own words, that no one could distort. After jotting down some thoughts, I ran the statement by my mom and Ben and reached out, as well, to Stephanie and Emma. I knew I could count on them even if I was no longer a White House employee. They were still my friends.

Emma made an excellent suggestion. I was going to put something in about "the amazing memories and friends I gained along the way." She explained why that might not be such a good idea. "I think friends/memories opens it up," she texted, "to more reporters trying to call those friends to ask what those memories were, unfortunately."

Speaking of friends, Hogan had sent me an extremely thoughtful text earlier that day:

> I'm so sorry about this, Madeleine. These people are hateful and disgusting and have attacked in a malicious way. You're in my prayers.

Look, I wasn't naive. I realized that more than friendship motivated Stephanie, Emma, and Hogan to help out. They had a very important job to do, and that was to protect their boss, the president of the United States. The more negative articles that were written about me and what I said, the more it could damage the president.

I passed along every inquiry I received from the reporters. I couldn't believe the lies they were coming up with. On second thought, I could.

One reporter claimed that, according to his "source," I had bragged on a visit to a Trump property early in his presidency that I could do "pretty much whatever I want because" Donald Trump found me physically attractive.

Similar to the Lippman text, that was so personal that I had to respond. The conversation he was referring to had never taken place, I told him.

Stephanie also weighed in. "I have never heard any of that," she emailed the reporter. "Can the press not just leave this poor girl alone."

Not every journalist was a disgrace to his profession. One, whom I will forever be grateful to, sent me an unbelievably warm text. After telling me he had some information about my resignation, he explained why he didn't need me to make a comment.

> I have decided that your day has surely been horrible
> enough and that this is not in the public interest to
> report all of these gossipy details about a 29-year-old
> who has a future career and no position of public power.
> We will simply aggregate the New York Times piece. I
> wish you the best.

I was blown away. If only other reporters in DC had been as decent.

★

I worked hard on my statement, and it wasn't merely to get the word out to the public. The audience I was most interested in was an audience of one.

I wanted the president to know that unlike some others who had left the administration, I wasn't about to go off the deep end and savage him in public.

That morning, I made the same point over the phone with Emma and Mick. You have my word, I assured them, and please make sure you pass it around the West Wing: I will not trash the president.

Why would I? I cared deeply about him, and being forced to quit was not going to alter that in the slightest. Furthermore, I knew how difficult it must have been for him to absorb what had happened. That's why he and Mick, from what I was told, had gone back and forth the whole day about whether I'd have to leave. The president couldn't believe that, of all people, "my

Madeleine"—that was how he often referred to me—would ever say something that devastating. Not after the loyalty I had shown him and his family. Perhaps if I had made similar comments about someone in Congress or the administration, I would have been reprimanded but allowed to keep my job.

This was different. This was his own flesh and blood. The president loves his family. He had no choice but to let me go, and I respect him for that.

Also, I knew the man himself. I knew how upset he could get when the people he trusted turned on him. It had happened over and over, and when it had, he had gone right back at them.

Being so vulnerable, the last thing I could afford was for him to lash out at me. Look at the others he had gone after when they attacked him upon leaving the administration. None had been a match for his wit, and, as everyone knows, there is no coming back from that.

Once everyone weighed in, I was satisfied with my statement. Only I didn't send it out right away. I began to think it might be better to keep my mouth shut. Why give the press another reason to come after me?

In the meantime, I went to work on step two, which was even more important.

Putting out a statement on the internet, if I were to do it, wouldn't be nearly enough. I needed to apologize to the president directly. I sent one text after another to my former colleagues in the building, asking if the president would accept my call. There was no guarantee that he would. Not so soon, anyway. Yes, he will, I was told. He will speak to you briefly before he heads to Camp David for the weekend. Expect a call in roughly thirty minutes.

I went to my room. As grateful as I had been to have Mom around those past two days for moral support, I needed to be alone.

Over the next thirty minutes or so, I did very little but wait. I was so paranoid about missing the call that I held my phone in my palm, staring at it, almost willing it to ring. The minutes felt like hours.

Finally, the familiar White House number came up. I couldn't help but be struck by the irony: for more than two and a half years, I had placed more calls on behalf of the president than anyone else, and now I was on the other end of that same connection, of what would undoubtedly be the most memorable phone call of my life.

The first voice I heard was Nick Luna: "Madeleine, I have the president for you."

# CHAPTER FOUR

# I'm Sorry, Mr. President

I was ready. I hadn't written down any talking points. All I would need to do was speak from the heart. The only thing I told myself, over and over, was: Madeleine, do not cry. If ever there's a time to be strong, this is it.

Seconds later, I heard the voice I had heard so many times, the voice I would hear from time to time in my dreams.

So much for not crying.

"Madeleine," he asked, "what happened?"

Great question. I wish I knew.

Almost an entire year has gone by, and I continue to ask myself the same question over and over and over. It's occurred to me lately that I may never know the answer.

"I'm so sorry, Mr. President," I said, sniffling away. It was the first of a half-dozen apologies, maybe more. I think I was trying to set a record.

"Were you drinking?"

"Yes, I was."

"Madeleine, Madeleine, this is going to be devastating for Tiffany."

Amazingly, despite the tears, I held it together for the most part. I didn't blame the press or ask for sympathy. I simply kept apologizing.

"Sir, at some point in the future, if you think it's appropriate, I would really love to apologize to Tiffany."

"Maybe later, but not right now."

The president spoke softly the entire time. He didn't appear angry, and I was greatly relieved, though I probably could have handled it if he had been. It wasn't as if no one had ever been angry with me. However, he was obviously disappointed, and that was worse. It broke my heart. Donald Trump was not my father, but he had become much more than simply my boss. I cared deeply about what he thought. I had always wanted him to be proud of me.

Before long, I could tell that the conversation was coming to an end. I told him how grateful I had been to serve in his administration and how much I loved him and his family. I said I was sorry one final time.

"I forgive you," the president said, "and wish you well." I have no doubt he meant every word.

We hung up. The call, which had lasted less than five minutes, was over, and just in time. When my mom, who had been listening from the stairway, came in, I started sobbing, and it felt as though the tears would never subside.

Looking back, when I spoke to the president was the first time I realized that my career in the White House was over. Somehow, in the back of my mind, I had expected the president to say that it was some huge misunderstanding and he would look forward to seeing me at my desk in a few days. The dinner in Bedminster would be behind us, this time for good.

Like everyone else, I have apologized to many people over the years for many mistakes, some more hurtful than others. It has never been easy, but nothing comes close to apologizing to the president of the United States.

I was also apologizing to a father whose children had been hurt—and not by just anyone, mind you, but by someone he regarded as a member of the family. The president had never expressed it in so many words—that's not his way—but I had a pretty good idea of how he and his children felt about me.

In June, we had been at the rally in Orlando where the president kicked off his bid for reelection when Jared said to a former member of the White House staff, "Madeleine is part of the family now. We can really trust her."

I was blown away. Feeling the connection was one thing; hearing it from Jared, quite another. I felt exactly the same way.

So what did I do with that precious trust? I threw it out the window, that's what.

Which, going back to what the president said on our phone call, prompts the question: Why?

To blame it completely on the alcohol is shirking my responsibility, and I refuse to do that. No matter what state I was in that night, I made the comments.

So again I ask: Why?

The only explanation I could come up with at the time was that I was trying to humanize the president, to show that he and his family were just like any family, with their own struggles.

If the media stopped for a minute to realize that, perhaps they would give the first family a break. If that was my intention, I went about it in the worst possible manner.

The comments I'd made about Tiffany made the least sense to me. As someone who had suffered from an eating disorder, I was the last person in the world who should bring up another woman's body. I know how tough women can be on themselves. They don't need anyone else to pile on the criticism.

I grew up dancing, first strictly ballet and then contemporary dance, and was preoccupied with being thin. Each time I looked in the mirror, I saw weight that didn't exist, except in my own mind.

I assumed I was so damn clever, hiding the disease from my family and friends. I restricted the amount of food I ate, and what I did eat, I often couldn't keep down, going to the bathroom immediately after meals. Everything about it was exhausting, but there was nothing I could do.

Eventually I saw a therapist, and it really did help for a while. The eating disorder came back in college and became so glaring that several friends staged an intervention at my apartment. I was mad at them, more ashamed than anything, but I realized later that it might have been the most caring thing anyone had ever done for me. I'm much healthier now, though there are times when, like every other woman, I still stress about my body, especially when I'm under intense pressure.

Besides, I considered Tiffany, just three years younger, to be a friend. We had gone to dinner once and texted back and forth many times. She often asked for my advice on what outfit would be the most suitable for a certain event at the White House, sending along some photos.

The president loves Tiffany very much. She was attending law school in DC, and he was grateful to hear I was looking out for her.

As awful as I felt about hurting the president, I felt worse about hurting Tiffany. He could handle it. He has been a public figure since the 1970s. That isn't the case with Tiffany. Unlike other members of the first family, she has chosen to stay out of the spotlight, which is her right.

So what happens? Someone she knows, a "friend," comments about her personal life, to a group of reporters, no less, and now it is all over TV and the internet. With friends like that . . .

I texted her a few hours after I spoke to the president. Although he told me to wait, I couldn't help myself. "I am so sorry. I hope one day you can forgive me."

She never responded. I don't blame her.

★

Still in tears, I turned on the television. The president was about to speak to reporters before he boarded Marine One to Camp David.

I used to step out of my office and stand in the Rose Garden to watch him leave. It was another privilege of working there that I didn't take for granted. Seeing him from my couch in California, though, it dawned on me: I'll never stand out there again.

The president does these mini–press conferences on a regular basis, and you can hear the sound of the helicopter's rotor blades whirling in the background.

The staff refers to it as "going to gaggle." The president calls it "going to see the wolves." I like his description much better.

I could barely breathe as I watched the scene unfold. As well as the phone call had gone, considering, I was still worried about what he might say about me. The subject was bound to come up, the wolves on the hunt for fresh meat.

When it did, it was the most surreal moment I have ever experienced, to hear myself being talked about on national television—by the president of the United States! I could see how deeply affected he was by the situation. I couldn't blame him. Thankfully, he didn't lash out. The president told the press that he had just spoken to me, and that "she was very down."He went on to mention that I told him I "had been drinking a little bit."

Ouch.

Think about it for a moment. The whole world would now assume I was an alcoholic. Can you imagine anything more humiliating? He was, however, under the circumstances, extremely kind, suggesting that I was a good person who had done a good job and wished me well. I was grateful. He doesn't say nice things too often about people who betray his trust.

Since then, people have told me to look at the bright side, that he was giving me an excuse: she never would have said those things if she had not been drinking. Some consolation, even if it is true. Plus, knowing how much he dislikes alcohol made me feel even worse. His brother Fred, who suffered from alcoholism, died in 1981; he was only forty-two years old. The president brought him up quite a bit, most often when groups of children visited the White House.

Soon, the gaggle over, he was on his way, and so was I, headed to see my dad in Newport Beach, about ninety minutes up the coast. I had planned to take the train, but my mom wouldn't hear of it. Worried I might break down if I was alone, she drove me there.

That evening, thanks to my dad, I was actually able to get away from the nightmare for a while. The two of us, along with my stepmom, watched Sebastian Maniscalco, one of our favorite comedians, on TV. I laughed harder than I'd laughed in days, listening to him poke fun at the ordinary things in life. I vowed to stop feeling sorry for myself.

My resolve didn't last long.

The next day, when I went to visit my grandparents, I lost it again. That, I eventually came to realize, would be the pattern for the foreseeable future. For a moment or two, I would escape from the living hell I had built for myself, only to be thrust back into it by one trigger or another. It didn't take much.

Many of us who make a mistake and lose something we cherish can at least begin to heal without constant reminders of what we did wrong. In my case, though, the person I had wronged was in the news every day, and that wouldn't change for some time. There was nowhere to hide.

As for my grandparents, I only wish I could have handled the press as well as they did. When a freelance reporter showed up at their home in California after the story broke to seek a reaction to my dismissal, my paternal grandmother, whom I call Mamu, calmly told the man how fond I was of President Trump and his family. As Dad put it, I should have made her my press secretary on the spot.

Even so, when I thought of Mamu, with her poor hearing, having to put up with a reporter showing up at her front door to basically interrogate her, it broke my heart and made me furious. The woman is eighty-five years old. For God's sake, leave her alone!

I also felt guilty beyond belief. It was my fault that the reporter had been there in the first place.

He then made his way to my dad's house. Fortunately, when my stepmom realized that it was a reporter, she slammed the door without saying a word. I couldn't believe that was happening to my family. It was such an invasion of privacy.

★

That same Saturday, I put out my statement on Twitter. Enough with being concerned about what the press might say. I had lost so much already. What else could they take from me? The statement read:

> It was the honor of a lifetime to serve President Trump
> in his Administration. I will be forever grateful for the
> opportunity!

I was glad to let everyone know how I felt. It *was* the honor of a lifetime.

However, I wasn't the only person to weigh in that morning on Twitter. So did the president. I had a feeling he wasn't done.

> While Madeleine Westerhout has a fully enforceable
> confidentiality agreement, she is a very good person
> and I don't think there would ever be reason to use it.
> She called me yesterday to apologize, had a bad night.

I fully understood and forgave her! I love Tiffany, doing
great!

At first glance, the tweet seemed pretty straightforward, and
I was gratified to be forgiven again. It could have gone a different way. Yet, taking a deeper look, I couldn't help but detect a
threat in there somewhere. Why else mention a confidentiality
agreement? By the way, I never signed one.

Even so, the tweet, although it disappointed my father,
didn't bother me. It was as good as I was going to get, and for
the president to put in writing that he forgave me meant the
world to me. Dad didn't know him the way I did. I knew how
much the president was hurting.

★

So much went through my mind as I tried to make sense of the
week in late August and early September, the worst week by far
of my life.

I thought of how fortunate I'd been to be in California when
I'd spoken to Mick, my family nearby for comfort, DC and the
White House press corps 2,700 miles away. As awful as that
week had been, it could have been worse.

I hadn't had to endure what John McEntee had, escorted
out of the building without collecting his belongings. With my
luck, the press would have been right on my heels, snapping
away. (John, by the way, went back to work in the White House
earlier this year.)

I thought, as well, of the friends who had checked in right
away, some I hadn't heard from in years. It meant more to me

than they'll ever know. They told me to hang in there and that they were thinking of me.

Others wanted to know "Are you okay?" How was I supposed to answer that question? Of course I wasn't okay. I wouldn't be okay for a long time.

I also reflected a lot on the conversations I'd had with Jared and the president's son Eric, both of whom, thankfully, I had been able to reach in the first few hours. I hadn't wanted them to find out about it first on the news. I still felt, despite everything, that they were like family.

Jared and Eric were incredibly loving and understanding. It made me respect them even more. "We forgive you," Jared told me, "and I'm a big believer in second chances." I have spoken to Jared a few times since, and he's always been gracious.

I find it revealing that the people who should be most offended by the comments I made at the dinner, the president's family, have been the ones who have been the most understanding.

Don't get me wrong. Some of the people I worked with in the West Wing were also there for me.

Including Hope Hicks.

Hope, though only two years older, was a role model. She had been with the president since the start of the 2016 campaign. I was intimidated at first by her poise, beauty, and talent. There wasn't anything she couldn't do. I was crushed when she had left the White House in March 2018, and I'm thrilled that she's back on the team now. The president is lucky to have her.

"You are smart and strong and fabulous," Hope told me the day I resigned. She also texted me an inspiring quote from another HH, former vice president Hubert Humphrey:

It is not what they take away from you that counts. It's
what you do with what you have left.

There were countless others whose thoughtful words could
not have been more reassuring.

After receiving a note I sent him, Secretary of State Mike
Pompeo texted, "We miss you and love you. All the best to
you." He was including his wife, Susan, whom I'd also come to
know well.

I have many warm memories of the secretary, the most vivid
being an intimate dinner he and Mrs. Pompeo hosted at the
State Department. It was an incredibly special evening.

I will also never forget when he told me about a recent secret
trip to North Korea; he was then director of the CIA. By that
point, the trip had been made public. The head of the CIA was
opening up to me, an executive assistant. Incredible!

The way he described the trip, I felt as if he had been to the
moon. No one in his traveling party had been allowed to go
anywhere without being escorted by the North Korean officials.
I asked if he had ever been scared. No, he said, but the members
of the delegation had definitely been "on guard."

Another cabinet member who was very gracious was the
secretary of transportation, Elaine Chao, whom, like Secretary
Pompeo, I met during the transition period between the election
and inauguration. She spent ten minutes on the phone cheer-
ing me up. "Things happen," she said. "People make mistakes.
You're going to be just fine. Please let me know if there is anything I can do."

Perhaps nothing matches the text I received from Sonny
Perdue, the secretary of agriculture. "I wanted to thank you

for the kindness you have shown since greeting me at Trump Tower," it read in part. "I will miss seeing you in the White House and I believe the President will as well. This is my personal cell and if I can ever be of help to you in any way, I would welcome the opportunity to repay a friend. Best, Sonny."

Wow. That was the other thing that was painful about how abruptly my time in the White House came to an end: I never got the chance to say good-bye to the cabinet members and representatives in Congress to whom I had spoken day after day and grown to admire so much. I may never speak to many of them again. It felt like a death of a certain kind and still does.

I was humbled, to say the least, even if I wasn't sure I deserved their kindness. Not after the embarrassment I had caused the president and his loved ones.

Other former colleagues, such as Sean Spicer, the president's first press secretary, reached out. Sean, whom I had known long before I went to the White House, cracked me up, and I didn't think that was possible. Sean, you might recall, left the administration in the summer of 2017. He texted:

Keep your head up. You weathered almost three years, which, BTW, is 2.5 more than me. :)

Kellyanne Conway, counselor to the president, also sent a text:

Thinking of you.

I was thankful, too, for the support I received from Tucker Carlson, who went to lunch with me a couple of weeks after I resigned. The fact that he was even willing to be seen in public with me meant a lot. I figured that most people, especially anyone prominent, would want to stay as far away from me as possible. I felt that radioactive.

Tucker, a star on Fox News, and I spoke about what my next move might be. He didn't have any suggestions, though he mentioned a profession I should definitely avoid: his. "Don't go into the news world," he said. "It's a brutal world." I didn't need much convincing.

No one was more on my side than Tucker's colleague at Fox Sean Hannity.

The Left sees Sean as Satan. He's anything but that. I used to talk to Sean often, and we got along very well. He treated me as an individual, not as Donald Trump's gatekeeper, which is more than I can say for a lot of people.

Still, I couldn't help but wonder: Will he be there for me now that I no longer work closely with the president? Most people, even the best of them, blow with the wind in DC. Left, right, middle, it makes little difference; they will drop you in an instant if you no longer serve their purposes.

Not Sean. He was there for me in my darkest moment, a true friend. He spoke to me as he would to his own kids, explaining that the whole ordeal was merely a blip in my life and that it wouldn't define me. His texts read:

> Your future is bright. The media is just full of jerks. You got burned...be very very proud of all your great work. Learn what you can learn from this, and do NOT beat yourself up...

Was Sean right? Did I get burned?

Yes and no.

As I said before, I take responsibility for what I said, and that will never change. The four reporters who were at the dinner didn't force me to answer their questions.

On the other hand, I wasn't used to dealing with the press, and they knew it. Worse yet, they didn't care. As they were pouring the wine and I was offering them one juicy tidbit after another, did it ever occur to them, even for an instant, that they were taking advantage of me?

Then there's the matter of what they did with the information I gave them. Off the record means exactly that: off the record. It doesn't mean that you can tell one of your colleagues what was said and *poof*, you're off the hook.

People suggested that I should have known better than to trust them. As Stephanie put it that day in her office, "Remember, nothing is ever off the record."

Obviously, they have a point, but again, I wasn't a press person. I didn't ask what the rules were as I took my seat that night at the Embassy Suites, looking forward to some pasta and a lively conversation. Though a few days later, after I left the White House, I reached out to Hogan, who confirmed it in a text:

OFF THE RECORD. 100%. They agreed to it.

Yet except for Tucker Carlson and perhaps a handful of others, no one in the media, either television or print, took the reporters to task for violating one of the most fundamental tenets of their profession. It was as if this was now accepted as the new norm in journalism. No wonder the press receives such little respect.

To me, the more pertinent question remains: How did the story get out? Who told whom, when, and why?

I understand that answering these questions will never change the outcome, but it would still be nice to know who was responsible, besides myself, for the loss of my dream job.

I realized early on that I will never know for sure. For the longest time, whenever I spoke to someone who still works at the White House or used to work there, I heard a different theory. It's gotten to the point that I don't know who to believe.

One theory I've heard is that Phil Rucker repeated what I had said to others, with Maggie Haberman, the *New York Times* writer, eventually, finding out. It was Maggie, remember, who broke the story. Or perhaps Rucker shared the information with her directly. I was told that Maggie was upset that she hadn't been invited to the dinner and Rucker opened up to her because he wanted to stay on her good side. If that indeed is true, I have no idea why her opinion matters so much to other reporters.

Another possibility, and it hurts so much to even put it down on paper, is that Hogan, my friend, had played a bigger role than I thought originally. I would like to believe that wasn't the case, but all I know is what I was told. A few former colleagues said that Hogan had brought up what happened at Bedminster to others in the West Wing, who had then approached the reporters who had been at the dinner for confirmation.

From there, the question is: How did Mick Mulvaney hear about the dinner? Did Maggie tell him? Or did somebody else in the White House tell him? Word in the West Wing spreads like wildfire.

Mick, according to one of those colleagues, later confronted Maggie for running the story, to which she supposedly responded, "I heard it from your own staff." Mick, I was told, promptly apologized to her.

I haven't asked Hogan or Mick if any of this is true, and I never will. Nor will I ask Phil Rucker or Maggie Haberman to confirm or deny anything.

Why bother? What they did to me was centuries ago in Washington time. They moved on right away. To their next scoop, their next casualty. I was old news before I knew it.

For them, I was the headline of the day, nothing less, nothing more.

Never mind that it was my career—my life!—they were toying with and that I'm still paying the price.

# CHAPTER FIVE

# Out of Hiding

I was tempted to remain in southern California, perhaps for a few weeks. Perhaps for longer. Close to the beach, far from the Beltway, surrounded by the comfort of my family, I could begin to heal. Who knew? I might even discover, much to my amazement, that there was actually life after 1600 Pennsylvania Avenue. Imagine that.

Maybe Sean Hannity was right; maybe being forced to leave the White House didn't have to define me.

I couldn't remain in hiding forever, of course. As Ben put it, I needed to get back to "our routine" as soon as possible. I loved my parents, grandparents, and sister, but Ben was a part of my family, too, and for better or worse, my life was in DC.

Our routine, prior to the trip to Bedminster, had been perfect. We'd wake up, get ready for the day, and go out and try to conquer the world—me in the White House, Ben in the Pentagon. Then, usually around 7:30, we'd meet back at the apartment, have dinner, and catch up on our favorite shows on Netflix. Many nights, we went out, attending one event after another. I could see that routine lasting for years.

We met, fittingly enough, at the White House in June 2017. Ben was there to have lunch with Chris, a mutual friend of ours, who served as the president's marine military aide. The MilAides, as they are known, consist of five service members, one from each branch of the military who carry the briefcase known as "the football," which contains the codes that would allow the president to launch a nuclear attack. At least one MilAide is with the president at all times.

Ben and Chris were walking on the colonnade from the East Wing to the West Wing as I was heading in the opposite direction. Chris introduced us. I was attracted to Ben immediately. Tall and handsome, with dark hair, he has the most charming smile.

A few days later, we saw each other again during a happy hour at a restaurant in Chinatown. A few administration staffers and the MilAides occasionally got together for drinks after work. I knew Ben would show up, thanks to careful scheming. Chris, who was like a big brother to me, had jokingly told me to never date a marine. He decided that Ben was an exception and was more than happy to play matchmaker.

Ben had no idea what Chris was up to. It was probably better that way.

"You need to come," he told Ben, who first said he was too busy. "Just be there."

Ben thought it over and decided that Chris must have a good reason for being so persistent.

We hit it off right away. It was such a relief to have a conversation with someone who was familiar with my world.

The guys I had previously met, once I told them I worked at the White House, were interested only in finding out more about my job. People in DC don't really care to learn anything substantive about you. What they want to know is: What do you do? Who do you work for? More precisely, how can it benefit them?

While on active duty in the Marine Corps, Ben was a military social aide in the previous administration. He served nearly eight years as a marine officer, which included a combat tour in Helmand Province, Afghanistan. What impressed me about him was that he could have started a lucrative career right after college, but he wanted to serve his country.

"Can I take you out sometime for a drink?" he asked after we had chatted for a while.

"No," I told him, "but you can take me out for dinner."

The words were out of my mouth before I could stop them. I had never said something that bold, surely not to a guy I was interested in and definitely not before our first date.

It said a lot about the confidence I felt around him. Ben brought out the best in me, as, I like to believe, I did in him. We started to date soon after that and moved in together about a year later.

★

Returning to our routine would be easier said than done.

When I boarded the plane for Baltimore on Thursday morning, September 5, exactly a week after the story had broken, I was a wreck. I worried that someone would recognize me, and if they did, they would say something mean. I had no idea how I would react.

In my mind, the entire world knew about what I had done, and the entire world hated me. Looking back, I was clearly overreacting. No one was thinking about me anymore. Yet it felt so real at the time.

People can be vicious. I knew that from reading comments on Twitter and Facebook about the president and other members of his staff. I never went looking for them, but they were impossible to avoid. Every time I thought some idiot in cyberspace had struck a new low for mankind, I was proven wrong. It's become so easy for people to hide behind a computer and say nasty things about individuals they've never met. No one will ever hold them accountable.

It was something else entirely, however, when the nasty comments were about me.

In the first few days after my resignation, my sister spotted a fake Twitter handle, something like @drunkmaddywesterhout. She thought it would provide a moment of comic relief. It didn't. I was horrified. Is this how I will be known for the rest of my life? As the woman who got drunk and lost her job in the White House?

My best friend became so alarmed by what she saw on the internet that she alerted my mom. "You need to have Madeleine deactivate her Facebook," she said, which I did right away. I also turned on the private settings on my Twitter and Instagram accounts. Tons of "follow" requests were coming in on Instagram and too many Twitter mentions to count.

I even wondered—and this further explains the mental state I was in—if there would be members of the press waiting when I picked up my bags in Baltimore. I wore a hat and sunglasses, just in case. I was relieved to see Ben waiting for me in the terminal, but I didn't calm down until we were on the parkway headed to Washington.

There was more anxiety ahead, unfortunately. As early as the very next day.

A gentleman from the Office of the White House Counsel whom I'd worked with in the past and a woman from Human Resources came to my apartment. They were there to give me the belongings that I had left in my desk and to take the items—a cell phone, laptop, iPads, badges, and other supplies—that belonged to the US government.

I was nervous, to be honest, which was why I asked a girlfriend to stop by for moral support. I was in no condition to go through the ordeal alone. However, they wouldn't let her stay in the room with us. Standard policy, I was told.

To prepare for their arrival, I spoke to an attorney. I didn't want to be caught off guard by anything the White House might ask me to sign, such as a confidentiality agreement, which, you may recall, I hadn't signed.

"They are going to act like your friends," the attorney warned, "but you have to remember they work for the administration. They don't care about you."

The lawyer wasn't kidding.

"Anything you might need, please feel free to email us," the HR woman said. "We are here for you."

Please. You have a job to do. You are not "here" for me. I didn't tell her that, naturally.

I signed the papers they brought, which seemed to be pretty routine, and tried to remain composed as I was what's called "read out" of my top secret security clearance. They reminded me that I could not share anything classified I had seen on the president's desk or overheard. That wouldn't be a problem. I knew the drill.

They then handed me the possessions I'd left in my desk, and that was when I began to cry. There was something about seeing my belongings stuffed into bags that felt like a punch in the gut. The wooden name plaque from Camp David. The rhinestone Diet Coke bottle. The trinkets I had collected over the years. And much more. I had spent so much time at that office it felt as if my entire life was in those two bags.

I thought it was over when I had apologized to the president and had thought so again when he'd sent out his tweet the next morning, but this was really the end. I had nothing left that belonged to the White House and vice versa. I almost felt as if I had never been there.

One of the possessions I would never see again was a lapel pin—the "hard pin," it was called—that I received from the Secret Service, which had allowed me to go anywhere the president went outside the White House without having to be swept by the agents. The pin, which I'd always known I'd have to return, had made me feel important. It was much more than a pin. It was a symbol of how far I had come.

Gone, too, was another object I valued, one of the three journals I kept during my time there.

Early on, my grandfather had suggested that I keep a record of my thoughts so that I could look back and remember how incredible the whole experience had been. It wasn't filled with state secrets—only names, dates, and memorable moments that would mean something to me and that I could one day share with my children and grandchildren.

I called Stephanie Grisham a few hours after I resigned to ask if she could take the journal out of my desk. I thought it was better that Stephanie, who is now back in the East Wing, working for the first lady, hold on to it than someone from HR or the Office of the White House Counsel. Unfortunately, I haven't gotten it back yet.

No one ever said anything official, but I always got the feeling it was frowned upon to keep a written record while you worked there. I believe it stems from the amount of turnover there has been in the building and the number of leaks the administration has had to endure. No one was sure who could be trusted. I jotted down some notes only when I was certain no one was around.

Anyway, after about a half hour, my two visitors left, and not a moment too soon. The HR woman gave me a hug at the end and said how sorry she was, as if that would offer some comfort. It didn't. It made me feel worse.

★

In the weeks that followed, I tried to go back to Ben's and my routine. Except the routine Ben had been referring to was gone—for good.

After he left for work, usually around 6:30, there were many days I couldn't get out of bed. Or I would move from the bed to the couch and then back to bed. I rarely set an alarm, thinking that I had no reason to get up at any particular time. I woke up at noon sometimes and still took a long nap before Ben got home in the evening.

Often, I didn't leave the apartment. There was nowhere to go. I didn't want to do anything or see anyone.

I watched as little news as possible—and, yes, that included the new hoax concocted by the Democrats and the press, the Ukraine investigation. When will they stop? The Democrats were so determined to impeach this president that they looked for anything that might stand up in a trial.

When I did tune in to see my former boss, I focused on the process, not the policy. Which was what I always did when I worked there. If, for instance, he was scheduled to speak at 3:00 but didn't start until 3:30, I was sure that he was either reviewing his remarks or talking to someone on the phone.

I would have placed that call. I would have told him he was running late. It felt strange to know what was, in all likelihood, going on behind the scenes in the Oval Office yet not be a part of it anymore.

I couldn't watch for long. It was pure torture.

Yet, as I did after the call with Mick, I knew I had to get busy. The final check from the White House would arrive in a few weeks. I needed a job. My parents suggested that I take several months off to process what had happened. It was clear to them that I wasn't ready to get back to work. For me, that wasn't an option.

Besides, as long as I kept moving, I could keep my pain at bay. It was always there underneath, believe me, but when it rushed to the surface, it overwhelmed me. I cried. I couldn't move. I asked the same questions over and over.

Getting out of the apartment, as hard as it was, was essential for my own sanity. Even if I went only to meet someone for coffee or lunch, I got dressed up and did my hair and makeup. It made me feel as though I were among the living, that I still mattered despite everything that had happened. I thought that if I looked okay, I would then *believe* I was okay, and others would believe it, as well.

Honestly, I didn't think finding a job would be that difficult. Surely, somebody in a town consumed with politics would hire a person who knew how this White House operated and maintained strong relationships with administration officials and major lawmakers. Former colleagues who had left the administration found excellent jobs without any trouble.

I took one meeting after another for weeks that fall. Every one went pretty much the same. "I can't believe what the press did to you," the people I met with would say. "We're really sorry."

I appreciated what they were saying, but I wasn't in the same place and wouldn't be for a while. Back then, I still felt that the debacle was entirely my fault. I couldn't stop beating myself up. Hearing over and over again how "sorry" people were made me feel even worse.

Besides, what I wanted from them was a job, not empathy. I got tired of having to explain to everyone what had taken place in Bedminster. I had gone over that night in my mind too many times as it was.

Fortunately, Jared came to my rescue. When he said to me on the day I left the White House, that he believes in second chances, he was sincere.

He called one day to see how I was doing. His call couldn't have come at a better time. He said he'd be happy to connect me with a few people. I thought about it for a while, knowing it was probably my one chance to utilize his connections.

Among those I asked for Jared's help with was Anish Melwani, the CEO of LVMH Inc., the North American subsidiary of Moët Hennessy–Louis Vuitton, the famous luxury goods company, whom I went to see in New York. I was willing to leave DC for the right job.

Maybe a fresh start in a new city would be exactly what I needed.

Mr. Melwani was very pleasant, as were others I met with, including a friend at Google and contacts at Oracle and Lockheed Martin. They were not the problem. I was the problem. My parents were right. I wasn't ready to go back to work. Not even close. A lot of people were willing to help me, but I didn't have a clear idea of what my next step should be.

To think that if I'd had been able to leave the White House on my own terms, I could have picked almost any job I wanted and earned more money than I had ever dreamed of. I would, in all likelihood, have been set for life and been on the right track to being offered many more rewarding opportunities.

Not anymore. I was damaged goods, that reckless woman who got drunk and betrayed the president of the United States. Who would want to hire her?

Everyone, I was certain, would be waiting for me to say something negative about the president—which I would never do, because I had nothing negative to say about him, or my experience at the White House. I was also concerned that wherever I landed, there would be a story about it in the news. That was the last thing I wanted—either for any company that would hire me or for myself.

My fears weren't based on reality. I was a long way from healing.

That wouldn't be easy, especially now that I was back in the District—not the scene of my crime, by any stretch of the imagination; rather, the scene of my success, and where I lived, a couple of blocks from the White House, didn't make it any easier.

For the longest time, I had felt fortunate to live in a building in the heart of the city, to go out onto the roof and see the president's helicopter land or take off. No matter how often I went up there, the view was always breathtaking.

It was also very convenient. If the president decided to come to the Oval Office unexpectedly on a weekend, for instance, and needed me, one of the military aides would call and I could be there in five minutes.

That was especially important in those early days, when we were not yet sure of the president's routine. Even when I knew he wouldn't need me in the Oval Office, being aware of where he was, at any moment, provided me with a tremendous sense of security. If I had to reach him, I would know the quickest way. If he was in the residence, I would call a certain number. If he was traveling, I would reach out to a certain person.

Now the fact that I lived so close felt like someone's idea of a cruel joke: let's put this woman through more agony, as if she has not gone through enough already.

When I went for a walk during those first few weeks in September, the neighborhood, with its four-star restaurants and corporate buildings and a Starbucks on every corner, seemed pretty much the same.

But it wasn't. Everything was suddenly, alarmingly different.

One minute, I'm sitting at my desk, five feet from the Oval Office, from the most important person in the world. I'm placing his calls. I'm arranging his meetings. I'm helping to make history.

The next, I'm sitting in my pajamas at one in the afternoon, worried about whom I might run into on the way to the grocery store. If, that is, I can get up the energy to even get out of bed. Every time I left my apartment, I had tremendous anxiety and it felt as though it would never end.

Before the dinner at Bedminster, my future had been set, and I was still in my twenties. Ben and I had talked about marriage. He had received permission from my mom to propose and would approach my dad next. Ben was excited.

So was I. I even started to compile a list of whom I would invite to our wedding. The president and Mrs. Trump, obviously, the rest of his family, the White House staff, and members of the cabinet and Congress. It was sure to be the wedding of my dreams.

Now, because of one night—one hour!—there would be no wedding. Not for a while, anyway.

Losing the job didn't just happen to me; it happened to both of us. It would take time and some serious reflection to truly understand what it would mean for us as a couple.

I would also need to ask myself some questions that had nothing to do with Ben and any future we might have together: Who am I away from the White House? Away from Donald Trump? I didn't have a clue.

I assumed I would work in the Oval Office until January 2021 and, if he won reelection, four years beyond that. The president, in fact, had been so convinced of that that he used to say, "Okay, Madeleine, six more years." I actually saw myself working for him after he left the White House, perhaps for his presidential library or for the Trump Organization.

Donald Trump won't be like other former presidents. He will remain in the spotlight, whatever he chooses to do, for the rest of his life.

Yet as the leaves started to fall and the Democrats kept focusing on Ukraine and the impeachment testimony, I was still in a great deal of pain. The slightest reminder—a text from someone I used to work with, the president's picture in the paper, the sound of his voice on television, you name it—would set me off, the memories flashing back, followed by tears, and questions. Always questions: How could I have been that stupid? Why did I even go to dinner with the reporters in the first place? Why did I keep drinking when I knew how much alcohol affected me? Why did I say things I didn't believe?

During the first two months after I lost my job, I refused to go down Pennsylvania Avenue. I simply could not bear the idea of walking past the White House. It's the most prestigious, recognizable building in the United States, if not the world. Everybody there had known me—the Secret Service agents, the residence staff, the groundskeepers, the military personnel . . . everybody.

In the past, when I walked down Pennsylvania Avenue, I loved to hear tourists speculate on whether President Trump was in his office or what he might be doing. It filled me with tremendous pride. I had been tempted to chime in: "Hey, everyone I know exactly what the president is up to right now. I work for him."

Every morning when I went in and every evening when I left, I walked through the East Wing and the ground floor of the residence. I took the same route the president takes, past the wonderful portraits of the former first ladies, past the Rose Garden, and into the West Wing. It was almost always empty, silent, allowing me to pause and reflect on where I was and who had been here before.

Unfortunately, I didn't gain closure with the building itself. I didn't get to pack up my desk and stand in the Oval Office one last time. I never said good-bye.

Finally, one day in November, I couldn't avoid it any longer. Ben and I were headed to a restaurant we enjoyed, and taking Pennsylvania Avenue was the most direct path. As we approached, I saw several dozen protesters in Lafayette Park. Naturally. There are always protesters across the street from the White House.

Suddenly, there it was, as beautiful and grand as ever. When working there, I don't think I ever really stopped to simply take in the magnificence of the structure, so consumed as I had been with getting to my desk and serving the president.

I didn't gaze at the building for very long that afternoon. It was more like a glance. I didn't want Ben to catch me. He didn't know it was the first time I had seen it since I left. After lunch, we walked past the White House once more, and again a glance was all I would allow myself.

Nor was I eager to run into anyone who worked there. I knew, however, that wouldn't last long.

One day, a former colleague walked past me as I was on my way to a Pilates class. I pretended I didn't see him, but he saw me. "Hey, Madeleine, how are you doing?" he asked.

"I'm doing okay, thank you," I said.

Mercifully, we spoke for just a few minutes, but it was precisely the kind of chat I desperately wanted to avoid. I didn't want people to ask how I was doing, to see the pity they felt for me. Nor did I want to have to lie, over and over. Lying requires too much energy.

The truth was, I couldn't have been doing worse.

# CHAPTER SIX

# *Blessing in Disguise*

Having had too much to drink, ironically, had been what led me on the path to the White House. It started that night at the sorority house in Atlanta where I was interning for the summer between my junior and senior years of college. The sorority meant the world to me.

Choosing the College of Charleston, a relatively small liberal arts school—there were roughly fifteen hundred students in my class—had made the most sense to me. I wanted to be as far away from California as possible. I felt it would be the best way for me to grow and explore a different part of the country. I had nothing against my native state, but I knew there had to be more to life than beaches and freeways and urban sprawl. The campus, and the city itself, possessed a charm and a sense of history I didn't feel back home.

In August 2009, when I arrived there, I didn't know a soul, and that was just fine with me. I was looking forward to living on my own, making new friends, and experiencing a new culture.

At the same time, I was hesitant about whether I would fit in with the southern girls, who are very different from California girls. I would need to trade in my Rainbow sandals and Abercrombie for Jack Rogers and Lilly Pulitzer. Women, by the way, made up about two-thirds of the student body.

As it turned out, I fit in just fine, and it was mostly because I decided to join a sorority, Alpha Delta Pi.

There were sixty girls in my pledge class. Those girls were exactly what I needed, instant friends. I hit it off with one girl in particular, Cathy from Atlanta. Cathy and I have remained best friends to this day.

Once the girls and I got to know one another—and it didn't take long—we embarked on an exciting new adventure, sharing our triumphs and trials: The first mixer. The first weekend on the town. The first trip to Sullivan's Island. The first everything.

Greek life was my whole life. I even thought I might work for the sorority after graduation.

Until the night in Atlanta.

I enjoyed some wine with the other girls I was interning with. We didn't get drunk, and, in any case, I was over twenty-one.

It made no difference. The rule was that there could be no alcohol in the house, period. Three other sisters and I were asked to leave the internship the next day. It didn't help my cause that I'd gotten into trouble with the sorority on a few other occasions back in Charleston, and given warnings by the executive board. But what college kid doesn't get into some trouble?

I was very fortunate to have Cathy as my friend. I was two thousand miles from home with nowhere to go. I'll never forget the kindness she and her family showed me when they picked me up at the sorority house. I don't know what I would have done without them.

Nonetheless, when I returned to Charleston for my senior year, I was confident that the executive board would simply give me another warning and I could prepare for rush. Nothing is as much fun as the four days of rush, girls going from one house to another. The sororities evaluate you, and you evaluate them. In the end, you pray that you find the right house. If you do, it can add so much to your college experience.

First, I would need to be judged by the board, which was made up of sisters a year younger than me together with a few older advisors. A hearing was set for the night before the first day of rush.

My mom made the long trip from California. She wanted to be there in case it didn't go well.

We met in one of the classrooms, sitting around a big table. I decided to make the others' job easier. I don't deserve to be the president anymore, I told them in a letter I read out loud. I was crying. I apologized for the mistakes I had made and asked for their forgiveness. I can think of only one other apology in my life that was harder for me. I left the room so they could deliberate.

Eventually, when I went back in, I could sense from how quiet it was that the punishment would be harsher than I imagined, and it was. Not only would I no longer be the president, but they were kicking me out of the sorority entirely. While the main advisor read the verdict, none of the other girls had the courage to look me in the eye.

I left the room and fell into in my mom's arms, sobbing. How could this be happening?

What now? If I could not be involved in Greek life, exactly what life was left for me in Charleston? The answer: none. I couldn't stick around; not in a school as small as this, where everyone seemed to know everything about everybody.

Students, I was sure, would point me out to their friends: "Look, there's Madeleine, the girl who got kicked out of ADPi for drinking. What in the world was she thinking?"

Sound familiar?

Instead, I decided to go home to California for the fall semester of my senior year. Mom and I figured out that with the credits I received for advanced placement courses in high school and the extra units I picked up in college, I could take a semester off and still graduate with my class in the spring of 2013.

For a long time, before I fell in love with the Greek life, my plan had been to go into psychology, which I declared as my major after freshman year. Due to my eating disorder, I wanted to learn more about myself and others who were suffering. The disease also impacts the entire family. I thought I could eventually help other young women with similar struggles.

After my sophomore year, though, I changed my major to political science. The advanced psychology classes were too science oriented, and science had never been my forte.

Besides, the summer before, I'd read a book, *Decision Points*, by former president George W. Bush that explained the crucial decisions he made in his personal life and presidency. I was moved by how candid he was about his mistakes and what he had learned from them.

Come to think of it, the two professions—psychology and politics—have a lot in common. Both require an understanding of what makes people tick, which has fascinated me forever, and nothing is more revealing than how our leaders behave under pressure on the grandest stage of all. What motivates them? What holds them back? What skills do they summon from within that can inspire us at the most critical times?

It wasn't as if I were a stranger to politics, especially the Republican Party. We lived in Orange County, a GOP stronghold since the dawn of time. Yet no politician had ever inspired me like George W. Bush. He is such a decent and honorable man, who always put his country first.

Like most people, I remember where I was that Tuesday morning in September 2001. Only in fifth grade, I was too young to know what the World Trade Center was, but by my mom's reaction to what she was watching on TV, I could tell that something awful had happened. As I got older, I came to realize what a remarkable job President Bush had done in responding to the attacks and keeping us safe for the next seven years.

My first venture into politics, actually, was in 2008, when I was the secretary of the Young Republicans club a friend had set up in high school. To call it a "club" is being generous. There were only about five of us, and if I am not mistaken, we met just a few times, though I still have the T-shirts we made. The front said, "NObama"; the back, "McCain-Palin 2008." I was very proud of how clever those shirts were.

I don't remember everything Senator John McCain stood for, but I knew he was for a stronger military and less government, and that was plenty for me. I was also turned off by how many other students—the entire school, it seemed—wanted Barack Obama for no reason other than he was for "hope and change" and that he was "cool." I bet you many of them couldn't have named a single policy, foreign or domestic, of Obama's that they supported. Besides, when did being cool become a qualification for the highest office in the land?

Then there was the issue of experience. Obama hadn't finished even a single term in the US Senate; John McCain had been a member of the Senate since 1987. He had spent five and a half years as a prisoner of war in North Vietnam while he was serving in the navy.

Going against the trend in 2008 brought out the nonconformist in me. I wasn't willing to blindly follow the crowd. More than a decade later, I'm still not, and that's why I often feel as if I'm on another planet when I'm talking to people my age.

In their world, everything should be free: free college tuition, free health care, you name it. They don't believe you should have to work for anything, and whatever makes your life easier is better no matter what it costs. No wonder they root for Bernie Sanders.

In my world, you work for everything. I'm sure it comes from seeing how hard my mom and dad worked, from as early as I can remember. They told me that they both landed their first jobs when they were only fifteen.

Dad, who grew up in a family of doctors, has been in health care his entire life, first as a respiratory therapist, then transitioning to sales and clinical education. Everything he does is determined by what is best for the patients.

Another important lesson I learned from Dad is that money and fancy job titles aren't everything. I admire him for always maintaining the right balance between work and pleasure. It's easy to forget that a job doesn't have to define you. I think the job he is proudest of is being a father, embracing the role of "ballet dad" and "cheer dad" when Katie and I were growing up.

Mom is no different. She gave up a successful career working in sales for a medical device company to have kids, but, after the divorce, she had to start working again. She spared no effort in supporting my sister and me. It wasn't until years later that I discovered how tough it had been for her. She knew the paycheck was coming on Friday, but often by Tuesday, she'd have no idea how she was going to pay for groceries for the rest of the week.

On a couple of occasions, she pulled up to our house, and when the garage door did not open, she knew the electricity had been turned off because she had forgotten to pay the bill. Trying to juggle a full-time job, manage the household, and take care of all the finances while raising two young children was very difficult. She also learned to balance her work and personal life, making sure to never miss an important moment in my childhood. Eventually she became a consultant for a pharmaceutical company and put her finances in order. She has done well enough in her career that she's retiring this year, well before turning sixty. I couldn't be more proud.

Mom was an ideal role model, as was Dad. It's no wonder that when I turned fifteen, I applied for my first job, as a lifeguard. I have pretty much been working ever since. It didn't occur to me that not having a job was an option.

★

In the fall of 2012, Barack Obama was on the ballot again, running this time as the incumbent against Mitt Romney, a former governor of Massachusetts. I knew about as much about Romney as I had about McCain.

No matter. I applied for an internship on his campaign. It was bound to be more rewarding and exciting than working for someone in a local race.

Several days later, while I was driving, the intern coordinator from Romney's office called. From the questions she was asking, I realized it was my job interview. It was hardly the best time to present myself, but I suppose I did okay.

"We want you to come work for us," she said.

Wow! This is fantastic, I thought. I will be able to work for Governor Romney here in California. It will be perfect for my résumé, and I will be able to spend time with my family on the weekends.

Or maybe not.

"How quickly can you get to Boston?" the intern coordinator asked. "We have a lot of work to do, and there isn't much time."

Wait, why Boston? I thought the job was in California.

As it turned out, the Romney campaign didn't have an office in Orange County. California was a state the Republicans couldn't possibly win in November. I suppose I had a lot to learn about politics. Off to Boston I went. I had only been home for about two weeks.

Nonetheless, I was excited. I would be living in a new city, in a part of the country I didn't know, working for someone who could very well be the next president of the United States.

NObama!

Only being an intern on a presidential campaign was nowhere near as glamorous as I'd imagined it would be. With ten other interns in my department, I spent the majority of my time in a windowless room, sifting through the emails people had sent through the campaign's website. Our assignment was to pick which emails required responses and which were considered hate mail. They kept us busy, that's for sure.

There were thousands of emails and phone calls, as well as numerous handwritten letters from average Americans, sharing what had happened to them and their families since Obama took office in 2009.

It was awful.

Lots of folks also sent coins, pictures, rosaries, and other personal possessions. I felt bad because I think they honestly believed the items would go to the candidate himself, not to interns in their early twenties to be recorded and filed away.

On the weekends, we went to New Hampshire, a state that, unlike California, would be up for grabs—to knock on doors. We asked people whom they planned on voting for in the presidential and local contests. I didn't enjoy it. I kept worrying that someone would yell at me or slam a door in my face. As it turned out, Obama would prevail by 40,000 votes.

Even so, I was working on a presidential campaign, and I could not have been happier. I needed something good to happen in my life. Getting kicked out of the sorority had been a huge blow to my self-esteem.

Besides, I was working on a *winning* presidential campaign. There was no doubt about it. One day, Chris Christie, the popular New Jersey governor, came to the office to address the troops. Governor Christie didn't say *if* Mitt Romney would become president. He said *when*. We believed him.

I know, everybody who works on a campaign thinks like that. I guess you have to in order to put in those insanely long hours, day after day. Yet the way the country was going, we had a reason to feel that way, especially after the first presidential candidate debate in Denver, when our guy performed better than Obama.

As the weeks went on, I asumed more responsibility, including being the key holder of the autopen. I took the assignment very seriously, perhaps too seriously. The autopen is the device used for a person's official signature. Once the governor was elected president, we certainly wouldn't want fake Romney signatures to be floating around everywhere.

Soon it was election day, and I was more convinced than ever: White House, here we come!

I called my mom around 5:00 p.m., a few hours before the first polls on the East Coast were set to close. "Everyone is excited here," I told her. "It's going to be such a great night. We have worked so hard to make this happen."

She tried to set me straight right away. "Madeleine, you know he is going to lose, right?" she said. "That's what everyone is saying on the news."

"What are you talking about?" I fired back. "He's not going to lose. There's still a lot of time left. The polls haven't even closed yet."

Mom turned out to be right, as usual.

The day, in fact, had gotten off to a horrible start. A special app we were pumped about, which would track voter returns, didn't work from the second the polls opened. The campaign spent hours trying to fix it, to no avail. Talk about your bad omens.

In the end, we carried almost as many states as Obama, 24 to 26, but he carried California, Pennsylvania, New York, Florida, and Illinois which had a total of 153 electoral votes. You need 270 to win.

Another four years with the Democrats in the White House. I was crushed. Perhaps not as crushed as the staffers who had devoted many years to the governor, on this campaign and others, but crushed nonetheless. No one had ever told me losing could hurt this much.

The next day stands out even more than the night before. Sometime in the late morning, I opened the blinds in the apartment I was subletting, and there was snow everywhere, the first real storm of the season. Perfect: a bleak sky to match my mood.

A friend called to let me know that the governor and his wife, Ann, were coming to headquarters to speak to the staff. I arrived just in time to hear Governor Romney finish his remarks. It was Ann, though, who moved me to tears. Before, whenever I had seen her on television, she appeared glamorous, refined, in total control. Not this time. Her eyes were puffy, and she didn't seem to have any makeup on. This, I told myself, is what defeat looks like.

★

Soon I was back in California and back to thinking about what happened with the sorority. The more I did, the more furious I became.

I hadn't changed my mind about my role in the dismissal. I broke the rules—just as I would later be the one to make the mistake at that fateful dinner in Bedminster. Only the rules should apply to everyone, and that clearly wasn't the case. It turned out that a group of women on the executive board had enjoyed some dinners of their own at the house in Atlanta and, yes, downed their share of adult beverages.

I wrote a letter to the president of the Grand Council, explaining the obvious double standard. I was fearless, and I believe it was because of the confidence I had gained in Boston. If the people running the Romney campaign hadn't considered me a disaster, surely the people running a *sorority* might want to take another look.

The council's response arrived in the mail within days: "Your membership has been reinstated."

You probably think I would have been elated and immediately return to the Greek life I cherished.

Not exactly. Alpha Delta Pi, with all its rituals and rules, didn't mean what it used to mean to me when I got back to school in January, and wouldn't ever again. Not after I had discovered my new passion: politics. George W. Bush's book had first gotten me thinking about this most promising world. Working for Governor Romney had made it official. I decided that after graduation in May, I would head to Washington.

In the meantime, I didn't abandon the sorority altogether. I went to a few of the meetings and several mixers. It was awkward. The girls who had voted to kick me out, who couldn't even look me in the eye at the time, would not say a word to me. Of course, I didn't have much to say to them, either. I realized there were more important things than being popular in a college sorority. Besides, I was busy working as an intern on another campaign.

The candidate was John Kuhn, a local attorney, who was vying to replace Congressman Tim Scott in South Carolina's 1st Congressional District. Scott had taken over Jim DeMint's seat in the US Senate when DeMint became the president of the Heritage Foundation, a think tank in DC.

Kuhn was one of sixteen candidates in the Republican primary in March 2013. No doubt, whoever won the primary would prevail in the general. A Democrat hadn't won in that conservative district since 1978.

I assumed a much larger role than I had in the Romney campaign. I participated in staff meetings, and supervised the volunteers. Kuhn could afford to pay them, while the other candidates couldn't. I didn't necessarily agree with his doing that, although it helped bring in additional bodies, including a few sorority sisters.

Ultimately, though, I got to experience again what it feels like to lose. I can't imagine ever getting used to it.

The seat went to Mark Sanford, a former governor, which made the outcome much harder to accept. Sanford is the man who had a relationship with an Argentinean woman while he was in office. He was married at the time, which was bad enough. He also misled his own staff, telling them he was hiking the Appalachian Trail; they couldn't track him down for almost a week, only later discovering that he had in fact been in another country.

I couldn't believe that somebody with such little character could win.

★

On May 11, 2013, I did what countless young men and women have done at the College of Charleston for decades. Instead of the traditional cap and gown students at other schools put on, I wore a white dress and carried red roses—the men donned white dinner jackets—and crossed through the legendary Cistern Yard.

Four years earlier, on my first day on campus, with many others, I had passed through the arch at Porter's Lodge. Written in Greek on the arch were the words "Know thyself." I can't pretend I did back then. I was eighteen years old. I knew almost nothing about myself or the world. So much had changed for me during those four years. I had discovered what I wanted to do for the rest of my life and how to stand up for myself. I was also proud of having left the comfort of California for a place that was alien to me.

Did those years have their challenges? Of course, and, as the evening in Atlanta proved, I made my share of mistakes. What I know now, though, is that everyone makes mistakes in college, and that shouldn't be held against you. Each mistake offers a chance to learn more about yourself.

I came to another important realization that spring of 2013, and I am more sure of it today than ever: getting kicked out of the sorority was the best thing that ever happened to me.

# CHAPTER SEVEN

# *A New Start in Washington*

I arrived in town the first week of June. It wasn't my first time in DC. In the spring of 2005, my mom, sister, and I, along with our nanny, Ashley, had visited as tourists.

I don't recall too much, except that we made the usual rounds to the monuments and Arlington National Cemetery while the cherry blossoms were in peak bloom. The Jefferson Memorial was especially stunning, surrounded by an array of beautiful pink flowers reflecting off the water of the Tidal Basin.

One day, we were walking around looking for a place to have lunch when we turned the corner and, presto, there it was, the White House. We walked right up to the fence and posed for pictures. George W. Bush was the president at the time. Even then, I was in awe of that building.

My plan in 2013 was to have a job lined up in advance, but that's almost impossible without being in DC for an in-person interview. Instead, I started as an intern for Congressman John Campbell from Orange County. He was a Republican, naturally.

Mom had a colleague who knew him, which helped push my résumé to the top of the pile, and, like most congressional offices, it preferred to bring in someone from the district to help out in the summer.

The internship would be a placeholder. I had done my share of them and needed to find a job where I got paid. My parents offered their support, and I had some savings from jobs in college, but living in this city can get awfully expensive.

Lonely, as well. I didn't know anybody, so I lived with four older girls in a house near American University. It was quite a contrast from living with my closest friends in college.

That, however, quickly changed.

The beginning of summer was the perfect time to explore the city with friends I made through my internship, who were also starting their own careers and trying to navigate that new environment. We hung out in rooftop pools, attended concerts, and went to every happy hour we could. I learned that one of the best ways to build relationships in DC was to grab drinks after work.

Meanwhile, I interviewed for jobs on the Hill. That's Capitol Hill for you outsiders. No disrespect to Hill staffers, but I soon discovered that it was not the life for me. I grew so bored answering the phone that I volunteered as often as possible to give Capitol tours to constituents, anything to get out of the office.

The tours were a lot of fun. I met the most interesting people, and showed them the Rotunda, along with the architecture and art that make the Capitol a unique and fascinating building. I loved stopping by the statue of President Ronald Reagan, so everyone could pose for a photo with a legend from back home.

Within a few weeks, I received my biggest break to date.

It began when I interviewed for the job of scheduler for Congressman Sam Graves of Missouri, who still occupies the seat. Unfortunately, the job required owning a car, which I didn't possess, to escort the congressman to meetings throughout DC. There was no Uber in those days.

The woman who interviewed me, however, mentioned a friend whose boss was looking for an assistant. She connected me with her friend, and we met for lunch at a restaurant on the Hill.

I passed the audition. The next step was a formal interview with her boss, Katie Walsh, the finance director of the Republican National Committee, the RNC. Everything in DC is known by its acronym.

For days, taking the advice of the RNC staffer I had met with, I read any article I could find about the committee and its chairman, a man by the name of Reince Priebus, and a report the RNC had put together after Romney lost to President Obama in 2012. I felt as though I were back in college, cramming for an exam. When it came time for the interview, I was prepared.

Katie, however, didn't ask me many questions about Priebus or the report. She was more interested in whether the two of us would be able to get along and work well together. If the first meeting was any indication, the answer was a definite yes.

Katie must have felt the same way, because a week later, she offered me the job. I'll never forget where I was when she called, in the basement of a large congressional office building. I said yes immediately. The salary was $32,000. That was pretty good, believe it or not, by Capitol Hill standards. Most entry-level jobs paid only $20K, maybe less.

I would end up working for Katie for almost four years. We got to the point that we could almost read each other's minds. She became more than a boss; she was a friend and mentor. I honestly don't know where I would be today without her.

The same goes for my feelings toward Reince. I didn't get to know him very well at first, not until Katie became his chief of staff after the 2014 midterm elections, but once I did, I found that he was a loyal boss who championed his staff.

The party was lucky to have him. Reince was willing to put in the work to turn things around. Every day, no matter what else was on his schedule, he spent three or four hours on fund-raising calls. He explained where the money would go and why we needed it today, not in the next quarter or next year.

Once the primary season was well under way, Reince had to convince donors who supported a candidate who had dropped out that the party still needed their help. You can't imagine how difficult that is. "This isn't about one candidate," he would tell them. "This is about the future of our country."

With Mike Shields, the chief of staff before Katie, Reince had heeded the painful lessons from 2012 and upgraded the party's flawed infrastructure. That's why we won back the Senate in 2014 and kept control of the House. The next, and toughest, challenge would be to regain the White House in 2016.

It wouldn't be easy. The Democrats would nominate Hillary Clinton, that much was clear. Whatever we thought of her, and it wasn't much, she would be a formidable opponent. People didn't call it the Clinton Machine for nothing.

What was far from clear was, of the seventeen candidates, whom the Republican party would nominate. It wouldn't be Donald Trump, that was for sure.

In the beginning, almost no one at the RNC, including Reince, took Trump very seriously. He was considered a sideshow by the establishment, who would fade away once the adults in the party stepped up, people of high character with experience in government, such as former Florida Governor Jeb Bush and Senator Marco Rubio. Besides, we needed somebody youthful and vibrant to draw a sharp contrast with Hillary, who would be sixty-nine on election day. Not another old white guy.

At least, I hoped Trump would fade away. He came across as a foul-mouthed womanizer.

Personally, I favored Senator Rubio. In 2015, at a donor retreat in Florida, I heard him speak in person for the first time. I was incredibly inspired by how his family had arrived from Cuba and achieved the American dream. He spoke with passion and conviction and was precisely what the party was looking for. No doubt he could beat Hillary.

Only, as we soon found out, he was no match for Trump. Not a single one of the other candidates was. Next to him, they appeared small, insignificant.

I felt bad for the senator when Trump kept referring to him as "Little Marco" and, worse yet, benefited from the insults. In his view, no one was off limits, including Jeb Bush, although Trump, I must admit, pegged him perfectly. Bush is extremely intelligent but doesn't have much charisma. He is not his brother.

While serving as the liaison between the committee and the various campaigns, I saw a lot of the candidates up close. One of my main responsibilities was to make sure they all had what they needed to prep for the debates. As you might remember, there were a lot of debates in the 2016 cycle and a lot of candidates, as there would be with the Democrats in 2020.

To work with the campaigns was a wonderful opportunity, though each had its unique requests. One campaign demanded Scotch tape and a certain kind of pen in the dressing room. Another a bowl of ice, another Diet Cokes.

In every debate, there was some controversy that had to do with the hold rooms, where the candidates waited before entering the stage—the greenrooms, as they are called in Hollywood. We made the assignments based on how the candidates were doing in the polls. Donald Trump almost always got the best hold room and whoever was at the bottom of the polls, the worst.

The most memorable controversy was during the third debate, which took place at the Coors Event Center in Boulder, Colorado, in late October 2015. This time the hold rooms were the locker rooms used by athletes, and they smelled exactly the way you would imagine.

Everybody was furious, and I couldn't blame them. You try prepping for a moment that could change your life, stuck in a cramped, stinky locker room.

Fortunately, the candidates and their aides didn't hold that against us for long, and I was able to forge trusting relationships with someone from each team.

Okay, not each team. Not Team Trump.

The Trump campaign, comprising much of the president's family, rolled into each debate venue as an entourage more than a campaign staff, and it was intimidating. They took pride in being the outsiders, and after almost four years in office, they still embrace that role.

As stressful as those debates were, we made sure to balance work and fun. We arrived in each city a few days ahead of time to finalize details for ticket holders and to ensure that the candidates received everything they needed. Once the work was done, though, we found a fun restaurant to have a team dinner.

Soon it was mid-July, and we were at the convention in Cleveland, Ohio. Four years before, I had watched the Republican National Convention on television. Never could have I imagined I'd be there. There is no better example of our democracy at work, except for the election itself.

Normally, there would have been no drama at this stage of the process, the nominee already decided. Yet nothing was normal about the election in 2016. Not until the balloons fell from the ceiling at Quicken Loans Arena was the battle truly over.

It's safe to say that I wasn't very excited about our nominee, and where our party was headed. Still, while I sat in Katie's box during the final night of the convention, it occurred to me that I was witnessing history so I may as well enjoy it. It would be a long four months until the election.

Which it was, although if you are a professional, you put aside your personal feelings and do your job. I learned a lot about responsibility and integrity from my parents and grandparents.

Another wonderful example was Reince Priebus. Whatever his personal feelings were, he made certain that the committee backed each candidate equally during the nominating process, giving each whatever he or she needed to succeed. He told us from the start, "You work for the party. Do not put anything on social media for any candidate. We are neutral until we have a nominee."

The moment Trump secured the nomination, Reince was there for him 100 percent, and so was the entire RNC staff—until about a month before the election, that is, when another Bush made an unanticipated entrance into the 2016 campaign. I'm referring, of course, to Billy Bush.

I don't need to repeat what Donald Trump said in 2005 to Bush, a radio and television show host, on the infamous *Access Hollywood* tape. You have probably heard it before. I will tell you that I was mortified, as so many others were.

Who talks like that? I couldn't believe that my party, the party of Abraham Lincoln, Theodore Roosevelt, and Ronald Reagan, had, as its standard-bearer, somebody who would use that type of language in describing members of the opposite sex. Mr. Trump seemed, I was afraid, to be exactly the man I'd thought he was.

The question for the RNC became: Is there any way we can get him off the ballot? We checked into it, but it was too late. The absentee ballots had been sent out.

Still, I'm not revealing state secrets when I say that Reince urged Trump to drop out. Many Republicans felt the same way. The future of the party, not just one man, was at stake.

Not surprisingly, no one came forward to defend the nominee—no one, that is, except Rudy Giuliani, the former mayor of New York City. He went on the Sunday talk shows, and for being on his side during the lowest moment of the campaign, he earned Trump's eternal, unwavering loyalty. That's who Trump is. He has been hurt so many times by people he trusted that when somebody comes through, as Rudy did, he will remember it for the rest of his life.

I saw that loyalty to Rudy countless times in the White House. When Rudy would say something way off the mark, a group of us would march into the Oval Office and practically beg the president, "Sir, you have to tell Rudy he can't go on television anymore. He is embarrassing himself and the administration."

The president wouldn't hear of it. "He is the only one who stood up for me," he'd say. "Rudy is my guy." You have to admire that. A lot of people, at the first sign of trouble, would bail, no matter how loyal that person had been. Not Donald Trump. Not ever.

Yet during that final do-or-die stretch of the campaign, for us at the RNC, it made very little difference what Rudy said on those Sunday shows. In fact, we canceled our scheduled trip to New York the week after the tape surfaced, as we still weren't certain Trump would remain the nominee.

People tend to forget how precarious that week really was. Talk about an October surprise!

He survived, needless to say, and soon we went back to work as if nothing had happened. It wasn't difficult. No matter what I thought of Trump, he was the candidate the party had chosen, and it was my job to help him become our next president.

All I can say is thank goodness for the coordination between the campaign and the RNC. The campaign had the energy, passion, and grassroots support. The RNC had the infrastructure, money, and strategy. Without that combination, Hillary Clinton would be in the White House right now, there's no doubt.

That doesn't mean we were always on the same page. Far from it.

What the Trump campaign did across this nation in a relatively short period was remarkable, even historic. Team Trump, however, didn't have experience running a national campaign. I'll give you an example. It may appear minor, but I assure you, it spoke volumes.

We were in New York getting ready for a meeting about the ground game and data operation. Katie had put together a presentation filled with detailed graphs, charts, and pictures showing how to collect people's data—name, address, phone numbers—and what to do to make them matter in November. I'm biased, to be sure, but I thought it was a brilliant representation of the hard work we'd been doing.

I can't stress enough how crucial the ground game is. Getting voters to back your candidate is one thing. Getting them to show up at the polls is something else entirely. Now we had to convince the campaign to give the ground game and data collection the same emphasis. That would not be easy. Having gotten as far in the process as it had without our help, it was wary of the establishment. The establishment was what it was running against, so why mess with a winning formula?

In one meeting, we asked the team how it was collecting data at the rallies that were drawing massive crowds.

"We're not," an aide remarked. "We don't have to. We know they're going to vote for us."

We were aghast. You're not collecting any data on those people? How are you going to target them? You want to win this thing, don't you?

Anyway, we worked on Katie's presentation at Trump Tower until the very last minute. It needed to be flawless. Finally, we were ready to go.

Only there was a problem: the Trump campaign didn't have an industrial-sized printer/copier in working order. I'm not kidding.

Time was running out. The major players—Eric, Jared, Kellyanne, Steve Bannon, and the others—would be there any second.

So I used the kind of printer that you buy for your home office from Staples—three, to be precise, each printing a single page at a time. I kept handing out pages to everyone in the meeting, then rushing back to the printers to pick up more.

Fortunately, in the end, we got our message across, and it made a big difference.

★

At last, it was here: November 8, 2016, election day. I had begun to think it would never arrive.

The day itself wasn't as hectic as you might assume. We had done all we could in the days and weeks and even years leading up to it. Now it was time for the American people to weigh in, including yours truly.

I walked to my polling booth on Capitol Hill and closed the curtain. I wasn't prepared. I had been so preoccupied with my duties at the RNC that I hadn't stopped to consider who I was going to vote for.

One thing I knew: it wasn't going to be Hillary Clinton. Hillary is corrupt to the core: Exhibit A, the Clinton Foundation. She and her minions also stole the nomination from Bernie Sanders, and I was still furious at her for calling the Trump supporters "deplorables."

What disgusted me the most was how Hillary, when she was first lady, had treated Monica Lewinsky. I know she needed to defend her husband, but she could have done it without attacking Monica.

Which left only Donald Trump, right?

Unfortunately, for me, it wasn't that simple. I was still having a difficult time getting behind a man whose values didn't seem to align with my own. I wrote in another name—another Republican, of course—and I choose to keep the identity of that person to myself. Which is my right.

There, I've confessed. I had hesitated for the longest time

because I didn't want to risk upsetting President Trump, and I still fear he won't be pleased to hear I didn't vote for him. He is fixated on the Never Trumpers and can be very hard on those who didn't support him from the beginning. That is even more the case for some in his inner circle. They see everything as black and white, which, I believe, is misguided and can be dangerous.

What they forget to take into account, and that is because some of them are not from Washington, is that if you're a political person and a Republican, at some point you probably supported the Bushes or Mitt Romney or John McCain. It doesn't mean that you're a Never Trumper.

After all, prior to 2016, Donald Trump had never been on the ballot. He himself was once a supporter of Mitt Romney and most likely other Republicans before him.

Besides, people have a right to change their minds. Don't they? Isn't that the freedom that we've been fighting for since the founding of our nation?

Whomever I voted for in 2016 is irrelevant. What matters is how I felt about the president once I got to know him, and I couldn't love and respect him any more than I do. I am ashamed to say I had believed everything that I saw or read in the news, and now I realize how foolish that can be, especially when the press presents only one side of the story.

I will vote for him in 2020. I will knock on doors—which, as you know, I don't particularly enjoy—and put up yard signs if he asks me. He was the right man to lead this country four years ago, and that is still true today.

It's safe to say, though, that I wasn't feeling great at RNC headquarters on election night as the results poured in, and it became increasingly clear that Trump would pull off the upset.

I was in shock, to be honest. I recall standing in the doorway of a conference room, leaning against the wall, when the networks called it. I started to cry, and they weren't tears of joy. Again, I offer no apology. That's how I felt that night, and there is no reason to pretend otherwise.

Later, in July 2019, when the book *American Carnage: On the Front Lines of the Republican Civil War and the Rise of President Trump* by Tim Alberta of Politico was about to hit the shelves, I became quite concerned when I learned that the story of my crying on election night would be in there. I immediately went to Stephanie Grisham and Dan Scavino. I needed to get ahead of the story before it was too late. "I don't want what I thought in 2016 to affect how you view me now," I told them. "Besides, you know how loyal I have been and how much I love the president."

Stephanie eased my concerns. "Yeah, we were all unsure of you RNC people at the beginning," she admitted, "but we know now that you're on the team."

Jared, as usual, backed me up 100 percent. "Don't worry about it," he said. "You're part of the family."

★

You might wonder: Would I have cried if Hillary had been elected?

The answer, though may surprise you, is no. Don't get me wrong: I didn't want to see that woman run anything, let alone the country I love so dearly. Yet at least I was prepared for Hillary to win. Everyone said it was a done deal, including many Republicans, and there was no reason to think otherwise. I wasn't prepared for Donald Trump to win. I'm not sure anyone was, besides Team Trump itself.

I got out of headquarters as soon as I could and called my mom on my way home. "I can't believe this," I said. "How could he have won? I'm quitting. I want to move back to California."

"Madeleine, you're exhausted," she told me. "It's late and you have been working nonstop for months, so don't make any decisions now. You're not thinking clearly. Go to sleep. We will figure it out tomorrow."

Exhausted or not, I was dead serious when I told her I was quitting. I had been thinking about leaving DC for a while. I came to Washington with high hopes and high ideals, only to learn that the place was as corrupt as people said it was. Money and power were all anybody cared about. I saw how much money influences politics early on, while working on the Hill and at the RNC.

It was also disheartening to watch politicians I admired not being true to their principles. The party members, for instance, who had called Donald Trump a threat to the nation's very existence, were often the same politicians who, craving power, now couldn't tell him often enough that he was the greatest Republican since Lincoln. Some were sincere, and I admire their change of heart. Others most definitely were not.

I thought that working in Washington, I would be surrounded by people striving to make the country, and the world, a better place. I know it seems naive, but I was truly surprised that wasn't the case. I became so disgusted that I made plans to apply for a position as a spin instructor in California. I had been going to spin class almost every day to help release the stress and pressures of the job. There, at least, I could do the kind of spinning that wouldn't make me ill.

I was in no hurry to get into the office the next morning.
I finally went in around ten, and when I got there, it felt as if
I had entered a whole new world. The place even had a different energy. Everyone else, including Katie, had been there since
very early in the morning.

No one at the RNC seemed to have a plan for what we would
do if Trump were to win. So I assumed that after the months of
late evenings and early mornings, we would sleep in and relax
for much of the day. Our work was done.

Quite the opposite. Our work was just getting started.

Call press conferences. Consult with members of Congress.
Meet with the transition team in New York. Go, go, go . . . We
won!

Even so, I couldn't bring myself to accept the new reality.
I spent the day, and the day after, in my office sulking, and I
wasn't the only person in the party with strong misgivings about
the new president-elect. Some victory.

Many, though, had spent years working for that very
moment, when a Republican would recapture the White House.
Now that all their work had paid off, it made no difference who
the Republican was.

On Thursday afternoon, Sean Cairncross, the RNC's chief
operating officer, a man I deeply respected, came into my office.
"Madeleine, what are your thoughts now that the election is
over?"

Well, Sean, as long as you asked. "Tell you the truth," I said,
"I want to leave. I don't want to do this anymore."

Sean looked at me for what seemed like an eternity. Then he
spoke and what he said changed my life. "I understand how you

feel," he said, "I really do. But you now have the opportunity to go work in the White House. You can't walk away from this. You have to give it a try."

He wasn't done with his pitch. "You worked extremely hard to be in this position," he said. "Are you now going to let someone else take that from you? Remember, it's much bigger than one person. You don't have to like the person, but to give up on the entire institution isn't an option. In the three years you have been in Washington, the Democrats have had the White House. It is now our turn to have everything. We are going to be able to do a lot for the country, and you can be an important part of that."

I thought for a while about what he said and realized he was right.

Ten minutes earlier, I had been planning my escape. Now I was fully on board. To be clear, I had not changed my opinion one bit about corruption in the nation's capital. Yet perhaps things would be different in a White House run by someone who was anything but a traditional politician, whose whole campaign had been based around shaking things up.

I owed it to myself to find out.

# CHAPTER EIGHT

## *Greeter Girl*

On Friday, three days after the election and a day after my chat with Sean, I went with Reince and Katie to New York to begin working with the transition team. When I said I was on board, I wasn't kidding.

On Saturday, we headed to Bedminster with the president-elect for the weekend. That was the first time I rode in a motorcade. What a blast. I sat in a black van, one of roughly thirty vehicles, and we blew through every light on Fifth Avenue as if we were drag racing on a deserted highway. If the girls from college could see me now!

The president, on a later trip, told me, "I haven't stopped for a red light in three years."

Several hours after we arrived, another aide and I helped out with a casual, celebratory dinner that the president-elect was enjoying with his team—Hope, Jared, Steve Bannon, and others—in the private dining room of the clubhouse. Our primary responsibility, as usual, was to make sure that Reince and Katie were taken care of. We stood toward the back of the room, out of the way, as you are supposed to do when you're a junior staffer.

Until we heard a familiar voice. "Come sit down and join us," Mr. Trump said.

"Is he really talking to us?" I asked the other aide.

We looked around, and there was no one else there. The president-elect was, indeed, talking to us. We cautiously walked over to the table and took a seat, as he'd suggested.

Although I don't recall every detail about that evening, I know I sat at the end of the long table, while the president-elect sat directly in the middle. He was in a great mood, recapping highlights of the campaign. I saw a side of him that I had not seen before but that I would see over and over in the years to come. The man loves to tell stories, and, given the amazing life he has led, there's a lot to tell.

As I listened, I was still in shock that he had asked us to join him. That had never happened with Reince when we had worked RNC gatherings in DC or on the road. Reince had been the principal, while we had waited in another room or outside. We were staff, not guests.

With that being the first occasion I spent more than a few moments in the president-elect's company, I began to won-der: Have I been wrong the whole time about him? Did I jump to conclusions by believing everything I saw on the news? Is he, dare I say, a good guy? From the way he interacted with everyone that evening, he appeared much more personable and charming than how he was generally portrayed.

It wouldn't be the last time he would ask me to join him for a meal, which may seem minor, but it meant a lot to me. He was warm and gracious every time. Unscripted moments like this revealed his true character.

The following day, back at Trump Tower, we got word that Reince would be the chief of staff in the new administration. Hallelujah!

It had never been a given. Steve Bannon, another influential advisor, had also been mentioned as a possibility, and Reince, after all, was seen as part of the establishment.

We were so proud of him. He had worked as hard as anybody else to put Donald Trump in the White House. I was very relieved. With Katie as his presumed deputy, I would likely be working with people I was familiar with from the RNC, many of whom were my closest friends. We had been through so much together over the last three years and were like a family. The fact that we were about to embark together on what promised to be a life-changing journey made it that much more exciting.

I knew the West Wing was bound to be an intimidating place, with turf wars and other petty conflicts. Having good, loyal friends by my side was sure to be a tremendous benefit.

Not everyone, as you might expect, was overjoyed. The RNC was a source of suspicion among Trump loyalists from the day in June 2015 their candidate rode down the escalator in Trump Tower and changed the party—and the nation.

Who are these people? they wondered. Why do they think, all of a sudden, that they are running the show?

Our view, naturally, was quite different. The president-elect's staff, we felt, had done a remarkable job during the campaign, but they needed to make room for us, as well. They were a little unsure of what they were doing—don't forget the printer fiasco—and there was a government to build.

The friction between the Trump insiders and the RNC, as a matter of fact, wouldn't disappear anytime soon. Even after Reince was appointed to his new position, he wasn't even given an office in Trump Tower.

Still, I was in working in New York City, and I couldn't have been more thrilled. I had come to the city a number of times since the convention, but this was different.

Along with a core group from the RNC, I flew in each Sunday night and took the train back to DC on Friday. We stayed in a hotel close to Trump Tower. Before long, I felt as if I knew the Big Apple as well as I knew Washington—at least the five or six blocks I walked every day. That was good enough for now.

Our most critical task in the early weeks was to set up interviews the president-elect would conduct for cabinet positions and other high-level posts. The presidential transition team had a long list of people it started to compile soon after the convention.

These meetings would, for the most part, occur in Trump Tower, the fifty-eight-floor skyscraper on Fifth Avenue between 56th and 57th Streets that had opened in the early 1980s. Walk around Manhattan long enough, and you are bound to pass it.

To get into Trump Tower, however, was no simple task. Not anymore. Not with the Secret Service surrounding the block and the massive crowds that were assembling every day. This was a busy area in normal times, but now that it was where the president-elect worked and lived until he moved into the White House, you can't imagine how many people gathered in the lobby and on the sidewalk.

I'd arrive every morning around eight, and the pool of reporters, which would grow to thirty or so, had started to set up in the lobby across from the elevator bank. Barack Obama was still running the country, but here, in midtown Manhattan, was where the news was being made.

Early the first week, Katie asked me to draft an email that, once she signed off on it, I would then send to the individuals who were coming in to interview with the president-elect. The email would include the date of the appointment, the time, and other pertinent details.

No big deal, I figured. I had set up countless appointments before.

How wrong I was.

In the draft, I suggested to the visitor that he or she meet me at the corner of 57th Street and Fifth Avenue, known as the Tiffany's corner. You can't miss it.

Call me when you are approaching the corner, I wrote, so I can look out for your vehicle. Most people, I assumed, would arrive in a car or taxi, not on foot. The corner would be crowded. Of course, every corner in New York is crowded. I'd then meet the person and from there escort him or her into Trump Tower.

Katie said the email was perfect. I hit "Send" and didn't give it another thought. Little could I have imagined that the one slight addition I put in on my own—meeting at the Tiffany's corner instead of inside Trump Tower—would end up landing me my dream job next to the Oval Office. I wish I could tell you that it was part of a calculated plan by a brilliant political strategist. It was anything but that.

All I did, really, was imagine how it might feel to have a job interview with the man who would soon be the president of the United States. I would be nervous, to say the least, and grateful to anyone who could help keep me as composed as possible.

Instead of having to navigate the crowds and track down the right elevator, they would be able to walk in with confidence, cameras clicking away, like an actor on the red carpet at the Academy Awards. It didn't hurt, if I may be so immodest, that their escort happened to be a self-assured young woman—half their age, in many cases.

Imagine if I hadn't met the guests at the corner. They might have wandered around the lobby, not knowing where to go and unable to get past the security-guarded elevators. Showing up late for a meeting with the president-elect wouldn't make a good impression.

On the other hand, the special treatment they received from me might give them the exact swagger they would need to win over Donald Trump. The interviews didn't last long, thirty minutes tops. They'd better be on their A game from the start.

The first interview took place exactly a week after the election. Right away, the walks to the elevator, which were more like processions, became a big hit. It was like a runway show every day. Friends and family members texted to say they had seen me on television. I was excited, but what really blew me away was the response I got from one viewer in particular.

The president-elect, I was told—who else could I have been referring to?—thought I had a good presence and a good walk. It was the first time I heard I had a good walk.

Presentation and look, you see, mean a great deal to Donald Trump, which comes from his years in television. Seems like a lifetime ago, doesn't it?

I will never forget seeing the first picture of myself online, with Congressman Tom Price, a Republican from Georgia, who later became the secretary of health and human services.

It was eerie. I realized that the press wanted photos of the president-elect and whomever he met with, but surely they wouldn't have any interest in me.

Yet, apparently, they did. Soon, I was given a nickname—two, as a matter of fact: "greeter girl" and "elevator girl." Greeter girl was used more frequently. I did not mind in the slightest.

I was introduced to the public, if you want to call it that, in a tweet by Howard Mortman, communications director for C-SPAN.

> BTW, if you've been watching C-SPAN #ElevatorCam
> non-stop and wondering who is greeting guests, it's
> Madeleine Westerhout, @madwestt of RNC.

Thank you, Howard. I owe you one.

It occurred to me that I was as close as I probably would ever be to true fame, and what person doesn't crave that at some point in his or her life? Before then, I had always been wary of being too proud of myself, even when I graduated from college or gotten the job at the RNC. Not this time. I was more proud of myself than ever.

Not everything people said, though, was flattering. Some poked fun at the fact that I'd been a fitness instructor, implying that I didn't possess any of the qualifications to work in politics. I was not just a fitness instructor but I'm proud that I taught Pure Barre on the side for a little extra money and to work out for free while I was at the RNC.

What bothered me the most, though, were the suggestions about how I had gotten the job. That I was the daughter of wealthy donors and had capitalized on their connections. Or, worse yet, that I must have slept my way to get it and was merely there for Donald Trump's viewing pleasure.

Some of the comments were too vile to repeat. It was incredibly insulting to me and to the president-elect. They couldn't imagine that a young woman might land a job because she happens to be smart and good at what she does and works extremely hard.

I had recently turned twenty-six, and ignoring the hateful comments was difficult. However, I was not about to let the things said by people I didn't know drag me down. I loved every minute I spent as the greeter girl. Getting to meet quite a few of the major players in politics and business was fascinating. It was a tremendous opportunity, one I could never have anticipated. I was determined to make the most of it. The huge smile on my face in the photos showed exactly how I felt.

I have always tried to present myself in the best way, but now I made a more concerted effort. I refreshed my lipstick and touched up my long brown hair before I headed to the lobby. As for my wardrobe, I couldn't afford to buy new dresses on my modest salary. I didn't work with a stylist or a makeup artist. Still, the show went on.

Then, as we hit the road, it was decided that I would play a similar role at Bedminster, where the president-elect spent weekends meeting with more men and women who might join his administration. Only this time, it was staged. Remember, we're talking about Donald Trump, the king of presentation.

Here's how it went: I would greet the individual coming in for the interview and take him or her to a hold room. I'd come back about thirty minutes later and lead him or her around to the front door of the building, giving the press the impression that the person had just arrived.

***Above left***: Trying on my first pair of pointe shoes  ***Above right:*** At my graduation from the College of Charleston in South Carolina in 2013  ***Below:*** With my friend Cathy in 2014 after our public tour of the White House

**Left:** Standing in front of the California delegation sign at the 2016 Republican National Convention **Above:** At the Ronald Reagan Presidential Library debate in 2015 **Below:** Playing "greeter girl," escorting Rick Perry through the lobby of Trump Tower (Photo Timothy A. Clary/AFP via Getty Images)

*Above:* At Mar-a-Lago, the first picture I took with
Donald Trump *Below:* With my parents and sister
at the inauguration of President Donald J. Trump

***Above left:*** Going over the president's schedule in the Oval Office (photo: D. Myles Cullen)
***Above right:*** Peeking out the window behind my desk to check on the setup of an upcoming event in the Rose Garden (photo: Shealah Craighead) ***Below:*** Taking dictation from President Trump (photo: D. Myles Cullen)

*Above:* Speaking with President Trump and President Macron after their bilateral meeting (photo: Shealah Craighead)  *Below left:* Boarding Marine One on the South Lawn (photo: Shealah Craighead)  *Below right:* With my boyfriend, Ben, on the West Wing colonnade, where we met

*Above:* With my grandma, Gammy, at the Kennedy Center *Left:* With my grandparents, Mamu and Grandpa, in the Oval Office *Below:* Checking the news in the Outer Oval Office with the president and vice president (Photo: Andrea Hanks)

*Above:* The vice president looks over my shoulder as I type up a statement at my desk (photo: D. Myles Cullen) *Below left:* At the Sheldrick Wildlife Trust in Kenya on the first lady's trip to Africa *Below right:* Always on the run (Photo: Joyce N. Boghosian)

*Above:* Christmas with my whole family  *Below:* With my closest friends in DC, Alex, Carrie, Andy, Lara, Mallory, Zach, and Ben

Meanwhile, Mr. Trump or a staff member would look out the window, waiting for me to walk up the driveway. The front door would then open at the precise moment the visitor showed up. The president-elect would greet the person, as I scooted out of the shot.

I could almost hear some director in the background: "It's a wrap."

For weeks, in Trump Tower and Bedminster and at Mar-a-Lago, Mr. Trump's private club in Florida, I escorted dozens of potential members of the incoming administration. I had never had so much fun!

Pick a prominent name in Republican circles—Mike Pompeo, Rick Perry, Rudy Giuliani, Nikki Haley, Newt Gingrich, Neil Gorsuch, and many others—I met them all. Once again, I got to see a different side of Donald Trump, although you'd never hear about it from the press. He met with anyone he felt could contribute to his administration and help the American people. It didn't matter that they had opposed him—Mick Mulvaney and former senator Bob Corker, for example—in the past. That's the point. It *was* the past, and the president-elect was turning his attention to the future.

He even met with Democrats, such as Congresswoman Tulsi Gabbard, Senator Heidi Heitkamp, and Senator Joe Manchin. Whoever it was, he couldn't have shown them more respect.

I liked most of the people I met; a few I did not. It often depended on whether they gave me any consideration. I could tell in thirty seconds, maybe less, who was genuine and who wasn't going to bother to give me the time of day. How you treat somebody who can do nothing for you is the truest test of character.

One person I liked immediately was Elaine Chao, the wife of Senate majority leader Mitch McConnell. She was friendly and took a genuine interest in me.

The first time I called her to talk about the interview—I also scheduled the meetings and put together briefings on everyone—she asked me where I was from, how I got my job, and how long I had been at the RNC. I felt as if *I* were the one being interviewed. She couldn't have been more kind, as she would be three years later, when I was forced out of the White House.

Jim Mattis, who would be appointed secretary of defense, was probably my favorite. I assumed that Mattis, a four-star marine general, would be stern and unfriendly. Not at all. He was a very sweet man, calling me "young Maddie." Later, whenever I saw him in the White House, he always had the same thing to say. "Maddie, I blame you for me being here," he would joke. "I was living a great life in Washington and teaching at Stanford until you called me one day." I laughed every time.

Several months after I left the White House, I called Secretary Mattis to see if he needed any help. The secretary was in the private sector by then.

"Are you planning on leaving your job, Maddie?" he asked.

He didn't know what had happened to me. How refreshing! I had assumed that everyone on the planet knew by then.

At any rate, I did my research on every person who was coming in for an interview. I knew which questions to ask and, perhaps more important, which ones to avoid.

For one person, however, research wasn't necessary. That was when I met the one and only Leonardo DiCaprio.

Leo is such a huge star that I couldn't take him through the main lobby at Trump Tower. He entered through the back, on the residence side of the building. The president-elect wanted everyone to come through the lobby and for the press to take note, but with Leo and a few others, he made an exception. Leo came to discuss climate change with Ivanka.

After their meeting, Ivanka brought him up to see her father. Once they were finished, I took Leo to a room to wait for his driver. I did my best to make small talk, asking how long he had been in the city. He was friendly, and after he told me he was hungry, I suggested he try the famous Trump Tower taco bowl. Just as I was about to get it, we got the call that his driver had arrived.

The nerve of the guy. My time with Leo went by way too fast. Unfortunately, I didn't get to ask him whether there actually had been room for both Rose and Jack on the raft.

Not every encounter with a celebrity went well. Another person I was excited to meet was Steve Harvey, the comedian and entertainer. The feeling went away in a hurry. He was not the charming person I saw on television, to say the least. He got really upset when I took him through the main lobby, as the president-elect had told me to do. Having to wait for an elevator in the crowded lobby for two minutes proved to be a huge inconvenience to him.

Nor was I infatuated with every politician or businessman I met, and that was a good thing. It kept me firmly where I needed to be, on Planet Earth. Somehow I wasn't nervous. I was just doing my job. When I was told, for example, to set up a meeting with someone from Kansas by the name of Mike Pompeo, I figured he was just another random congressman, one of 435. Sorry, Mr. Secretary.

One encounter that is memorable was with Rick Perry, the former governor of Texas, who became secretary of energy. It wasn't so much what he said as it was the picture of him holding on to my arm in Trump Tower.

People saw the picture and were offended, saying that the way he had touched my arm was inappropriate. Friends and family even asked about it later, suggesting that it must have made me uncomfortable.

Nonsense. We were having a wonderful chat when he reached over at the precise moment the photographers captured their shot, and he let go moments later. He was laughing because I had asked about his recent appearance on *Dancing with the Stars*. The haters will look for any reason to find fault with a Republican.

Later on, I would become quite familiar with the men and women who joined the administration. Having gotten to know them even just a little before they took office made all the difference in the world. We had a history together. When they arrived in the Outer Oval for a meeting with the president, we would engage in a casual conversation that helped them relax. No matter who you are, you're always going to feel a certain level of anxiety when you walk into the Oval Office.

Another meeting that stands out was with someone I was already familiar with, Mitt Romney. The former governor and the president-elect, as everybody knows, were not on good terms. During the campaign, Romney had blasted Mr. Trump, suggesting that if the Republicans were to choose him as their nominee, "the prospects for a safe and prosperous future are greatly diminished." Surely a statement that negative would disqualify him from a position in the Trump administration.

Or maybe not.

The two were set to meet in Bedminster on Saturday,

November 19, the speculation being that the president-elect might ask Romney to be his secretary of state.

I put a little extra effort into setting up that meeting than I usually did, even sending his staff a video of exactly where to stop their car. I wanted everything to go just right. I was working for Donald Trump now, but I still admired the governor a great deal and imagined what might have been going through his mind.

Only four years earlier, he had been the party's nominee, and now he was meeting for a job with someone from his own party who had been able to win the election. That must have been tough.

As for myself, who knows? If I hadn't worked on his campaign, I might never have made it to Washington in the first place.

In any case, the meeting between the two went off exactly as planned, which gave me tremendous satisfaction. They also met for dinner two weeks later in New York.

In the end, the president-elect didn't offer him the job—it had always been a long shot—but I still hoped they could put aside their differences and work together on issues where they found common ground. Unfortunately, it hasn't worked out that way.

★

On December 9, one month after election day, it happened. I brought Admiral James Stavridis to his interview, scheduled for 11:00 a.m. Admiral Stavridis, who was the dean of the Fletcher School of Law and Diplomacy at Tufts University, was being considered for secretary of state or director of national intelligence.

I did what I normally did, trying to make the admiral as comfortable as possible. We spoke for a few minutes before the president-elect was ready. I then took the elevator back to the

thirteenth floor, where the transition staff was located, to continue scheduling more meetings. We'd accomplished a lot in the
past three weeks, but there were still plenty of positions to fill.

Shortly afterward, Katie gave me a message: "The president-
elect wants to see you."

See me? For what? She wouldn't tell me.

"Don't worry," she said, seeing the nervous look on my face.
"It's good."

That didn't exactly ease my nerves.

When I got upstairs, in addition to the president-elect and
Admiral Stavridis, Reince was there, along with Jared and Steve
Bannon. I cautiously poked my head into Mr. Trump's office.

The president-elect said the admiral had been telling him
how hospitable I had been. Once he heard that, Mr. Trump
said, he wanted to share the compliment with me in person. "I
have seen you on TV," he went on. "You're doing such a great
job." It was the first time I could be certain that he knew who I
was. That wasn't the case at the dinner in Bedminster.

"Thank you, sir," I said.

That was the end of it, and it was enough. As I went down in
the elevator, I felt on top of the world.

★

Ever since the conversation with Sean Cairncross at the RNC,
two days after the election, I had assumed that I would continue
to be Katie's assistant. Never wanting me to settle for less, she
asked if I might want to work for an agency or get involved in a
policy matter I cared about.

No thanks, I told her. She was like an older sister to me and the best boss I could possibly have. Wherever she would go, I would follow.

Or so I assumed.

One day, shortly after my encounter with the president-elect, Katie asked me a question I will never forget: "Do you have any interest in sitting outside the Oval Office?"

"Umm, sure," I responded, not having the slightest idea what she was talking about.

She went on to explain that Rhona Graff, Mr. Trump's long-time executive assistant, wouldn't be moving to Washington. I would be given the opportunity to fill the position instead.

"Reince, Jared, and Steve all think it's a good idea," Katie said. "If you are interested, they will pitch it to the president-elect, and we'll see how it goes."

I was grateful to hear that Jared and Bannon had signed off on it, but no doubt Reince had been the driving force. Jared and Bannon didn't know me well yet.

Donald Trump agreed to it, but as the weeks dragged on, no one sat me down and told me exactly what the position would entail. No matter. I wasn't merely going to the White House; I would be working for the president himself.

It was incredible, really, no matter how it would come to an end, and when I reflect on my years in the West Wing, it occurs to me how easily it could have been different. As Katie's assistant, I would've been working in another part of the building. I would not have gotten to know the president the way I did, and I would, in all likelihood, have left the White House when she did, after only two months.

Thank God I was greeter girl.

★

# CHAPTER NINE

# Living the Dream

With Christmas right around the corner, I thought of the perfect gift for my family: a picture of myself with Donald Trump. I had pictures of me with everyone but the man himself.

Still, I felt uncomfortable about asking. I saw him pose for photos and sign autographs like you wouldn't believe. The last thing I wanted to do was add to that burden. Besides, the right moment never seemed to come up.

Until one day in the living room at Mar-a-Lago. We had just finished a meeting, and there were only a handful of people around. I realized this could very well be my best chance. Even then, I couldn't get up the nerve to ask him myself, so I asked Katie if she would make the pitch. No problem, she said.

"Sir, would you mind taking a picture with Madeleine?" she asked the president-elect. "She is too shy to ask you."

He couldn't have been nicer about it. "Madeleine too shy?" he said. "I don't believe it. You've been on TV for weeks now. You're not shy. Of course I'll take a picture with you."

We took the shot, which turned out so well that I made it into a New Year's card. My family was thrilled.

I then thanked him and walked away, thinking, yes, I was definitely wrong about this man. He's not the horrible person a lot of people say he is. It's amazing how different someone can be once you get to know them.

About a month later, on January 18, two days before inauguration day, I got another glimpse of the man you don't necessarily see in public.

We were on Donald Trump's personal plane—known as Trump Force One during the transition period—headed to Washington. Katie, who was already in DC, had asked me to secure his official signature for the autopen and for merchandise that would be sold in the White House gift shop, such as mugs, hats, and pens. Documents are placed on the president's desk constantly. He doesn't have time to sign every one. That's why you need the autopen, which I remembered from the Romney campaign in 2012.

I was very nervous. For the first time, I was around Donald Trump without anyone else from the RNC. The president-elect and the team that had been with him from the start didn't trust me yet. How could they?

I could almost hear the whispers: "Watch out for her. She's from the RNC."

The Trump loyalists and the RNC, remember, had been wary of each other since the early stages of the campaign. We had gotten closer at the convention in Cleveland and closer again when we had defeated Hillary. Yet there was still resentment when we arrived at Trump Tower to start work on the transition.

"Does Reince have his own RNC agenda?" Team Trump wondered. "Are these people, who were not with us from the beginning, going to be supportive of what Donald Trump wants to do for this country?"

You can see why I might feel I didn't belong. Yet I had no choice. All my RNC colleagues were in DC, preparing for the inauguration.

I took a breath and got out of my seat. No time like the present. As apprehensive as I was, there was something about the president-elect that made him very approachable. He looked totally at ease, sitting alone at a table, reading the newspaper and going through other paperwork. I asked if I could sit down. Sure, he said. I'd brought several pens for him to work with, and he took out a few of his own, which he likes to do at times.

He signed the piece of paper a couple of times with different pens, his signature in different sizes, and then slid the sheet back to me. In my possession was a single 8½-by-11-inch piece of white printer paper with what would become the most iconic signature in the world. Precious cargo, to say the least. I thought to myself: *Madeleine, whatever you do, don't lose this!*

Donald Trump was so friendly and gracious, which helped to calm my nerves. RNC or not, he made me feel that, yes, I did belong.

"Do you think you can handle the job?" he asked at one point. "Are you ready?"

I had my doubts, I will confess. I had yet to step foot into the White House, except for a public tour I had taken in 2014, which didn't really count. I had assumed that I would be trained for my job, but that wasn't the case, except for a brief meeting with Rhona Graff. In fact, no one ever told me who I would officially report to, and it would remain that way the whole time. Frankly, I had no idea what to expect.

Furthermore, until then, I had yet to spend a moment alone with the person who was going to be my boss. That's not the best way to start any new job, especially a job as intense as this would be.

Fortunately, I was smart enough to keep those doubts to myself. The president-elect wouldn't want to hear them. He had enough to worry about.

"Yes, sir, I'm ready," I told him. "I'm going to work really hard."

"Great," he said. "Thank you."

I went back to my seat as we were about to land.

★

Finally, it was the morning of January 20, 2017, inauguration day. My parents and sister were in town to share the whole experience.

I felt incredibly blessed. Mom and Dad had been divorced since the early 1990s, but they had always put my sister and me first, showing up for the moments that mattered most to us, and this was definitely one of them. I have many friends from broken homes where that wasn't the case.

Our seats in front of the Capitol were not the greatest—sorry, guys—with no view of the president-elect or anybody else on the dais, except on the huge screen. It was a cold and rainy day.

I didn't care one bit. We were about to witness history: Donald John Trump being sworn in as the forty-fifth president of the United States.

I listened to his speech, applauding over and over. I loved

when he said, "The forgotten men and women of our country will be forgotten no longer" and "We've made other countries rich while the wealth, strength, and confidence of our country has disappeared over the horizon."

It was about time we had a president say that. America first!

Even so, my mind was a million miles away, thinking about how, as soon as the ceremony was over, I would be heading to my new office—my new life.

Less than four years had gone by since I had arrived in this city with ambitions and little else, spending a lot of my time answering the phone and giving tours of the Capitol. Like other young politicos on the Hill, I had dreamed of working at the White House but had never expected that to come true.

*I've made it,* I kept thinking. *I've really made it!*

A stranger sitting in the row next to us asked how we had gotten our tickets and where we worked. I thought for a moment of telling him the whole truth but decided against it, simply saying we had received them from the RNC. There was no way he would believe I was really the president's executive assistant. I could hardly believe it myself.

Once the ceremony ended, I said good-bye to my family and rushed over to a government office building at the corner of 18th Street and New York Avenue, where the transition team was based. It was halfway across town.

To this day, I don't remember if I walked, took a cab, or hopped onto the underground Metro. I was so filled with anticipation that for all I know, I might have flown there.

After I was swept by the Secret Service and gave them my ID, I got into a van with about a half-dozen others for the ride, literally, across the street to 1600 Pennsylvania Avenue. This time, instead of taking pictures with my mom and sister outside the gates, I would be going in.

We came to a halt on West Executive Avenue, the private street between the West Wing and the Eisenhower Executive Office Building. It was almost 3:00 p.m., about three hours since the president had taken the oath. I went inside the Lower West Wing and was taken upstairs to the Roosevelt Room, where laptops and phones were laid out for us on a conference table. A man from the Executive Support Team gave me my equipment, and after turning on the computer and programming the iPhone to make sure that everything was working properly, he motioned for me to follow him.

"I'm going to take you to your office," he said.

My office! In the freakin' White House!

We walked across the hall to the Outer Oval Office. "This is your desk," he said.

The desk was smaller than I thought it would be, and so was the area around it. That was pretty much true about everything in the West Wing.

I don't know what I had expected, really. Perhaps I was thinking of what I recalled from watching *The West Wing*, the television show in the late 1990s and early 2000s that starred Martin Sheen and Rob Lowe. I loved President Bartlet and C. J. Cregg.

As I'd soon discover, the real West Wing is nothing like the made-up version. Actually, there isn't a movie or television show, to my knowledge, that has gotten the layout and the feel of the place quite right.

You would not believe how many doors and hallways you stumble upon. One can easily get lost. I can't tell you how many times I would be at my desk and someone would pop their head into the Outer Oval Office, asking "Is this the right way to the West Wing Lobby."

"No, it isn't," I would tell them. "Turn back around, and go all the way down the hall."

Speaking of doors, I asked my escort, before he left, about the one five feet from my desk. The door was closed.

"Is that the Oval Office?" I asked.

"Yes, it is," he responded.

"Am I allowed to go in there?"

"You can do whatever you want. This is your office."

Once he left, I put the laptop and phone onto my new desk and for the first time opened the door to the Oval Office, which was heavy and several inches thick.

It was empty. President Trump was at the parade. He wouldn't be here for hours. I looked everywhere, trying to take in every detail. I was in awe, really, the kind of awe you feel once or twice in your entire life, if you're lucky.

The fact that I was alone in the Oval Office my first time made it even more special. That moment will always belong to me, nobody else, and nobody will ever be able to take that away from me.

Soon it was over, as two of the president's valets, Waltine and John, entered the Oval to introduce themselves. Walt asked if I was hungry. You don't need to cater to me, I told him, that is not your job. He said he didn't mind, and, realizing I hadn't eaten all day, I gratefully accepted the turkey sandwich and chips he brought me.

I ate at my desk, the hours ticking away, the area around the Oval still to myself. I rummaged around in my desk to see what President Obama's former assistant had left there. I checked out the phones and toyed around with my computer. I tried to look busy.

Every so often, I wandered around aimlessly. The layout of the West Wing was very confusing. I wanted to learn my way around while the building was still quiet; I was sure that wouldn't be the case again anytime soon.

I visited the Navy Mess. The chief of staff's office. The Briefing Room. I went to every room I could find. There aren't that many. I was beginning to get my bearings, to grasp the subtleties of the place that would become my second home.

I also took time to check out the entry points into the Oval Office.

There are four doors into the Oval. One led into my office, another into the hallway across from the Roosevelt Room. A third opened up to the West Wing colonnade and Rose Garden, while the final door led to a small hallway and then to the president's private restroom, study, and dining room.

From my desk, there was another door to my right that led to the Cabinet Room. Around a long, oval-shaped conference table were leather chairs, one for each member of the cabinet. The president's chair, the back of which is about two inches taller than the rest, was in the middle of the table, not at the head, which is important; we live in a Republic, not a monarchy. Each chair also had a plaque on the back to indicate which member of the cabinet the chair belonged to. Only that secretary was allowed to sit in that chair. I loved pointing out details like that when people came in for tours.

A building is inanimate, that's obvious, but that does not prevent us from establishing a bond—with this building, especially, where Lincoln and Kennedy and the Roosevelts changed the course of history. If that does not inspire you, I don't know what will.

Later in the afternoon, other employees finally started to file in—each, I'm sure, relishing the moment like I was.

About an hour later, it was time for me to go. I went to the hotel where my dad was staying and we both got dressed for an inaugural ball at the Walter E. Washington Convention Center, one of many that evening. My mom and sister joined us. We mingled for a few hours, and then, near midnight, they arrived—the new president and new first lady—looking glamorous, ready to make history of their own.

As I watched them dance to Frank Sinatra's *My Way*, a song which could not have been more fitting, the gravity of where I would be working, and who I'd be working for, hit me once more: That's my boss!

★

I was back at my desk on Saturday morning. It never occurred to me whether or not I should come in. Weekend or not, it was the White House, and there was work to do.

As a matter of fact, in those first two or three months, I do not recall taking any days off, including Saturday and Sunday. I was not kidding when I said you don't have much of a personal life when you work there. Mind you, I am not complaining one bit. I recognize how blessed I was—now more than ever.

That first Sunday, the senior staff, which was comprised of roughly thirty assistants to the president—APs, as they are called—were officially sworn in.

I was reminded of how many were giving up lucrative jobs in the private sector to fight for issues dear to their heart. I can't begin to estimate what the difference in salaries was. Which is why I got frustrated when people who had stayed on the outside to make their millions, called the president from time to time to complain about a certain member of the administration. All it did was get him spun up about something that could have easily been avoided.

I felt like telling some of these critics, "Okay, you go sell all of your assets, and then see if you can do it better than we can."

At times, I felt guilty that I was earning more money than I had ever imagined making at the age of twenty-six.

Money wasn't the only thing they sacrificed. Some chose to relocate their entire family—in the middle of a school year, no less—while others left them behind, visiting just on weekends. That takes a huge toll on any family. I felt fortunate to be single and not have any kids.

The first day on the job that stands out was the following Tuesday. The president, not thrilled with the artwork in the Oval Office, decided to go on an unscheduled tour of the West Wing. He did it on several occasions the first few weeks.

Remember, President Trump made his reputation as a builder of many remarkable hotels, office buildings, and golf courses. To him, no detail is insignificant.

"I love that one," he would say, pointing to a painting on the wall. Within hours, the painting would be hanging in the Oval.

There were several pieces of modern art hanging on the walls then that were beautiful but not the president's style. He preferred portraits of former presidents and prominent American figures. His favorite is a portrait of President Andrew Jackson, the populist who served two terms in the 1820s and '30s. Donald Trump sees himself as the modern-day Andrew Jackson.

Under that painting is Frederic Remington's famous solid bronze *Bronco Buster* statue, which has been in the White House for more than a hundred years. Over the marble mantle of the fireplace is an exquisite portrait of George Washington.

Each time I entered the Oval Office, either to see the president or in the morning before he came down from the residence, I focused on something I hadn't noticed before.

Take the Resolute Desk itself. It is not just a desk. It is history.

One day, I looked closely at the panels that had been added to conceal the braces Franklin Delano Roosevelt wore due to his polio. I was also intrigued by the two-inch wooden platform added during Ronald Reagan's presidency. He needed the extra height so that his knees could fit under the desk.

The same fascination went for my observations of the entire room: The gold curtains from the Clinton administration on the windows behind the desk. The oval rug used in Reagan's two terms, designed by his wife, Nancy, that covered the hardwood floor. The busts of Abraham Lincoln, Martin Luther King, Jr., and Winston Churchill. The tiny circular indentations in the floor, which were cleat marks made by President Dwight D. Eisenhower's golf shoes.

One day, I looked up at the ceiling and noticed a medallion of the presidential seal. There was no end to the splendor of the Oval Office.

The president thoroughly enjoyed adding his own personal touches. When it was time, for example, to change the wallpaper, he went through books of different patterns, picking out the exact one he thought was most suitable for the Oval Office, as well as ones for the dining room and private study.

I used to hear him say all the time, "This is what I do. This is what I'm good at."

Still, the president didn't rely entirely on his own tastes, asking myself and his valets which patterns or pictures we preferred. I was always amazed at how he asked everyone around him to offer an opinion. That is how much he values people, no matter their position.

For me, it was another step forward in learning about the man himself, in realizing how wrong I had been about him. The kind, respectful way he treated everyone, from his military aides to his butlers, wasn't what I had expected, and it didn't start on the day he became president. I constantly heard from people who worked for him at his different properties: "Donald Trump is the best boss I have ever had!"

The president is convinced that he can learn something from everyone, and he has a way of making people feel valued.

As I was getting to know him, I was careful to remain in the background. He had enough people in his circle whom he'd known and relied on for years. He didn't need me to be assertive just yet. I had to learn my job first. If I couldn't do that properly, it wouldn't matter how well he and I might get along.

That first week, one of the toughest challenges was learning how to operate the phones. The White House phone system is quite complicated. People might call in on a nonsecure line, but the president wanted to get them back on a secure line, and, at first figuring out how to do that was confusing.

Once, while trying to transfer a call from a secure phone into the Oval Office, I was getting increasingly frustrated, and I wasn't the only one.

"Learn how to work these [bleep] phones," a voice in the distance said.

I don't have to tell you who it was.

"Yes, sir," I said, "I'm working on it."

On another occasion, a call came in from Rupert Murdoch, who owns Fox and the *Wall Street Journal*. Knowing the president was on the phone with Ivanka, I put Mr. Murdoch on hold and walked into the Oval.

"Sir, Mr. Murdoch is on the phone," I said. "Would you like me to tell him you will call back?"

He erupted like Mount St. Helens. "Never put Rupert Murdoch on hold!" he said. "Never!"

"I'm so sorry," I told him. "I figured you would want to finish the call with your daughter."

As it was, Mr. Murdoch was on hold for thirty seconds at most and would no doubt have understood if the president needed to call him back. He is the president, after all.

Yet to Donald Trump, Murdoch's time was valuable—as valuable as his own, even—and he wasn't an exception. The president was very respectful of other people's time, no matter who they were.

"How long ago did they call?" he always asked. "How long have they been waiting for me to call back?"

Now, you may think I'd be rattled to be reprimanded by the president of the United States. I wasn't. He would vent from time to time, but, unlike other bosses I've heard about, he let go of any negative feelings in a hurry.

Speaking of the phones, on my second or third day, the president asked me to track down President Obama so he could thank him for the letter he had put in the drawer of the Resolute Desk. It's a ritual for the outgoing president to leave some thoughts behind for his successor.

The letter was pure Obama, one sentence standing out: "Regardless of the push and pull of daily politics, it's up to us to leave those instruments of our democracy at least as strong as we found them."

I reached out to the operators in the Situation Room, and, believe it or not, they did not have a number for him. I assumed they had a number for everyone on the planet. I felt like saying "What do you mean? He was here in the White House just three days ago."

The two presidents were finally able to connect, though not for long, and if I am not mistaken, it's the only time they have spoken to each other since Obama left office. Donald Trump and Barack Obama, it's no secret, aren't exactly on the best of terms.

"Obama just sat here and watched basketball all day," the president used to complain.

Come to think of it, he isn't the biggest fan of George W. Bush, either. Often, after painful conversations on the phone with family members who'd lost a loved one in Afghanistan or Iraq, he'd hang up and feel incredibly agitated. Those conversations, I imagine, have to be the most difficult a president ever has to make, and they never get easier. "Bush got us into this," he would say.

I used to cringe whenever I heard President Trump, whom I admire greatly, speak like that about another man I also held in high regard.

Only, what was I to do? Tell the president he was wrong? I don't think so.

During my time in the White House, I hid my true feelings whenever the president brought up President Bush, while also looking for any chance to bring the two of them together. I was thrilled when the president reached out to him in July of 2018, when he was deciding whether to nominate Brett Kavanaugh to the Supreme Court. Kavanaugh had served as staff secretary in the Bush White House.

I placed the call, finding Bush on the golf course. I listened from my desk. It wasn't very hard. President Trump's voice carries. It would be difficult not to hear him. I couldn't believe how lucky I was to witness two presidents discuss a matter of such magnitude. Bush told the president that Kavanaugh would be an excellent choice and thanked him for the chance to weigh in.

Then, a year later, I saw an opportunity to bring Bush to the White House.

President Trump was to hold an event in which he would sign a bill funding the victims of 9/11. I suggested that he invite Bush. No, he said, without hesitation, making another reference to the wars in Afghanistan and Iraq.

So I let the matter drop, but only temporarily. I knew enough about him by that point to know he can change his mind. The key in asking him the same question a second time is to phrase it in a way so he doesn't *think* he's changing his mind, that it was his decision all along.

"I just want to make sure you don't want to invite President Bush," I said a few days later.

"Ah, go ahead and invite him," the president said.

I contacted the former president's office in Dallas. Unfortunately, he was unable to attend, although he appreciated the gesture.

A couple of times, I suggested that President Trump invite President Bush to play golf with him. The two don't seem to have very much in common, but golf is a passion they share, and I thought that perhaps a day on the links would establish a bond which would be good for both of them. It was a nonstarter, although I'm still hoping that one day the two might get together for a round. I'm sure they could learn a lot from each other and have a good time. From what I know about both men, they share a wonderful sense of humor. You need it in that job.

Every so often, I made other recommendations, which he actually empowered me to carry out. He realized that the more ideas that were presented to him, the better he could serve the country.

★

In March of that first year, I got to experience something else I had never imagined: I flew on Air Force One when we went to Florida for an RNC retreat.

By that time, the president's relationship with the party had grown much stronger, and it was bound to get even better with Ronna McDaniel as the new chairwoman. Ronna had been the party chief in Michigan, which had turned red in 2016 after going for Obama in 2008 and 2012.

I left the White House roughly ninety minutes before Marine One took off from the South Lawn. Once I got on board, I looked for my seat. Every seat has a little card with the name of the person traveling on it. While we waited for the president, I went exploring, as I had the first day in the West Wing.

I had never thought much about what Air Force One would be like, but I assumed it would be similar to any other airplane with regular seats: window, middle, and aisle. It's nothing like that. Think of it instead as the White House on wheels. The front stairs are reserved for the president and the first family, the back stairs for the staff.

There are tables with two and four seats apiece and an assortment of goodies—M&M's, chewing gum, bowls of fruit—everywhere. On long flights, the flight crew made popcorn as we watched movies. Air Force One is so gigantic that there is a full kitchen, an area with printers and supplies, and a doctor's office. I was told that minor surgery could be done there.

If you ask the president, you can sit anywhere in the plane you want. Once when he found out that his guests, mostly members of Congress, were seated in the back of the plane, he was beside himself. The next time and every time after that, they sat in the conference room or in the president's cabin. In his opinion, Air Force One is similar to the White House; it belongs to everyone, not just him. If you ask the advance team, you'll get a much different answer. I almost felt they were thinking "You guys might have the power in the White House, but we're in charge when we're on the road." They adhered to strict logistics, wanting you to remain in your assigned section of the plane for the entire flight. I was so anxious about going up to the president's cabin if I had something to tell him or if there was a call I felt he needed to make.

One day, Dan Scavino set me straight. "Madeleine, just go," he said. "You sit near him all day long and go in and out of the Oval. What's the difference here?"

The advance team relied on the past to justify their tight control. "This is how Bush did it," they argued.

That irritated me to no end, and I heard it more than once

from those who had served in the Bush administration or under President Obama, for that matter. I respected their way of doing things, but I didn't believe there should only be one way. Donald Trump proved that by how he ran his campaign and energized the Republican base.

I was often tempted to respond, "This is not the Bush White House or the Obama White House. This is the Trump White House, and everything that you thought you knew about working in the White House you should throw out the window. He does things differently."

In those first few months of 2017, I was learning more every day about the man in the office five feet away from me, and the more I learned, the more I respected him.

I was learning more about myself, as well. Aside from the two early mistakes—not working the phones properly and putting Rupert Murdoch on hold—I was doing pretty well. In just about every other job, you enjoy a honeymoon period. If you make a mistake, you don't lose sleep over it. Your boss understands. You're new here; you'll eventually get the hang of it.

Not this job. From the first day, no one got a pass. There was no one to say "Let me show you around" or "This is your job description." You sat at your desk and did the work. You had to just figure it out for yourself.

Everything was happening so fast, we didn't have the luxury to stop and ask ourselves: What are we actually doing? Instead, it was: We're here, and now we have to find the best way to make this work.

It might have helped to sit down with President Obama's assistant, but, since the transfer of power is so abrupt, that never happened, and that was true for almost all of my colleagues in the West Wing. We were on our own.

Yet, as the weeks, then months, went by and people came and left, those of us who remained took tremendous pride in the fact that we were the ones who had been there from the moment the president first stepped into the Oval Office.

We felt incredibly honored to serve a president who was, day by day, making America great again.

# CHAPTER TEN

# *Learning the Ropes*

I remember the first time I realized Donald Trump would be unlike any boss I'd ever had and, without question, unlike any president the United States has ever had.

It was late in the afternoon of January 25, only five days into his presidency. I was working at my desk, minding my own business, when all of a sudden there he was, standing only a few feet away, looking around the Outer Oval Office. He promptly took a seat in front of my desk.

*Oh, my gosh, what is he doing?* I wondered. *Does he need something?*

He didn't need anything. In between meetings, he was just taking a minute to say hello to everyone, to ask how we were doing. Simply being himself. We were still getting used to our new surroundings, and so was he.

It seemed the most natural thing in the world for him to engage in a causal conversation with us, without any agenda. He would pop in like that almost every morning when he came down from the residence and every night when he left for the day. Sometimes he would stop by just for a piece of candy.

On other occasions, the president would be in the Oval Office for a meeting, the door closed, when it would swing open and he'd emerge with a stack of papers for me to distribute or inquire about who had called in the last hour or so.

It always occurred to me that he could have simply picked up the phone. I should have to go to him, not the other way around.

Perhaps, but that's not Donald Trump. He was more than willing to come to us. He was the leader of the free world, yet he was making it clear that he was no better than we were.

Believe me, it mattered. It mattered a great deal. He made everyone feel respected and supported, eager to take on any assignment, glamorous or not.

Day after day, he asked the staff, "How's it playing?"

At first, I would allow someone else, such as Hope Hicks or Dan Scavino, to give him the update. They were monitoring events at home and abroad much more closely than I was.

After about six months, though, as I began to feel more comfortable, I took the initiative. "It's playing great," I said more often than not. "Things are looking good. You're having an excellent day so far."

Conversely, on days when things were not going so well, I chose my words very carefully: "It's not playing great, sir."

Never did I outright tell him that things were playing poorly. I left that to someone else.

As time went on, the president frequently wanted to know where he stood in the Rasmussen Daily Presidential Tracking

Poll, the poll he believed was the most accurate. Whenever his approval numbers were strong, I couldn't wait to deliver the news.

"Tweet it," he'd say when he was satisfied. "Put it out."

On the other hand, if the numbers weren't especially positive, in the low forties, perhaps, I would wait for him to ask. When I told him, his standard reply was "What happened?"

That wasn't for me to say. It could have been Iran, the border issue, the Russia investigation, the stock market; on any given day, any one of a number of reasons.

One decision I made early on, and I stuck to it the whole time I was there, was that if I didn't know the answer to a question he asked, I wouldn't make something up. "Mr. President, I missed that story," I would tell him, or "Sorry, sir, but I don't know enough about that subject. You should ask someone else."

I also refused to automatically go along with whatever he said, as others did. Okay, that wasn't entirely true. Once, when he brought up his good looks, all in good fun, I did go along with it. "Sir," I said, "yes, you are definitely the most handsome president this country has ever had."

The key was that I treated him like a normal person. It sounds ridiculous, I know. What I mean is that I respected him but I didn't hesitate to push back a bit if I felt it was necessary. If I had been nervous every time I spoke to him or walked into the Oval Office, I wouldn't have been able to do my job effectively.

Take, for example, the weekly two-minute videos that the communications team wanted to put out. The president often wasn't in the mood to tape them. The request typically came at the end of a long day.

"No, I don't want to do it right now" he would usually say.

"Okay, no problem." I would drop the matter.

A day later, I would bring it up again. Sometimes he'd say yes, sometimes no. When he said no, I let it go again—until the next day.

Finally, though, we would be running out of time to release the video and the team couldn't wait any longer. "Sir, I know you don't want to do it and you're really busy today," I'd say, "but it'll only take a few minutes, and then you'll be done for the day."

He'd agree, and once he got going, he'd do a great job, often recording four or five videos in one session.

★

Unfortunately, more often than not, people gave him answers when it was apparent that they had no idea what they were talking about. They were that desperate to please him. Except he knew precisely what they were doing; that's how intuitive he is. He even posed certain questions to staff members as a test to see who was telling the truth and who offered what they knew he wanted to hear. It never ceased to amaze me how aware he was of everything that was going on in that building. Nothing got past him.

If every time the president asked how things were "playing," a staffer told him, "Things are fantastic, sir," that was one person he could tell was lying. How, then, could he be sure that person was ever telling him the truth?

In my opinion, anyone who wasn't completely honest with him was doing a great disservice to the president and to the American people. For him to make the smartest decisions on issues, large or small, he needs to know the truth, however unpleasant it might be.

Which is another thing the press has gotten wrong about Donald Trump. He has no interest in being surrounded by a group of yes-men. If somebody disagrees with him, that is totally fine, but just telling him "That's wrong" or "You can't do that" isn't good enough. You need to explain *why* doing it isn't in the country's best interest.

If the reason makes sense, he may not be pleased. He may even take out his frustration on you, in person or in a tweet. Yet he will always listen.

A perfect example is the occasions when, at the last minute, he told us he wanted to attend a certain sporting event. There were several discussions about him throwing out the first pitch at an upcoming Nationals or Yankees baseball game.

"Sir, you can't go to the game," I told him. "The Secret Service hasn't had anywhere near enough time to make it safe for you." He understood completely. His safety and the safety of everybody around him were much more important than any single event.

Fortunately, weighing in on delicate policy matters wasn't my job. My job was to make sure the president got from one place to the next and stayed on schedule as much as possible. I was the one who kept the trains on the track.

At first, we had him starting his day in the Oval Office at 9:00 a.m. That didn't work.

"This is way too much," he told us. "I'm in the office from nine in the morning until nine at night. We have to cut this down." Twelve-hour days in the office, on top of the work he does in the residence, would be unsustainable for anyone.

From then on, his first meeting in the Oval Office would rarely start before eleven, and more often than not, his first meeting would be his daily intelligence briefing.

The staff would become frustrated when he sometimes didn't show up until 11:30 a.m. or even later. I could see their point, but it was not as if he was lounging in bed. He was actually up at dawn, reading the paper, watching the news, and making calls.

Then, once a meeting got going, you could forget about it ending on time. I always laughed when I saw a fifteen-minute meeting on the schedule. A fifteen-minute meeting will go forty-five minutes. An hour meeting will go an hour and a half. He believes in spending quality time with everybody, whether it's a four-star general or the head of a local union.

Of course, the meetings couldn't last forever. When he felt they were finished, he banged his hands on his desk twice with open palms. That was the signal. Most people got the hint and walked out rather briskly.

Not everyone did, however, and that's when I would have to go into the room to get things rolling: "Sir, we are ready for your next meeting." I had to interfere multiple times a day.

On some occasions, the door open, he wouldn't bang on the desk. He would give me a look and ask, "Madeleine, what's next?" or "Who called?" That was my cue to usher everyone out.

We were finding our way together, the two of us. One day, after the president had dictated a statement to me, he praised the great job I was doing. The word he used to describe me, and I will never forget it, was "treasure."

I can't overstate how much that meant. He hadn't picked me; his chief of staff had. We had spoken only a couple of times before the inauguration. The conversation on the plane when he signed for the autopen was the only significant time I spent with him before he became president. From day one, I tried to prove I was worthy of his trust. I don't think I ever stopped trying.

The president connects with people on a very intimate level, which I saw for myself every day. He would be in a meeting in the Roosevelt Room when, all of a sudden, he would blurt out, "You don't want to be in here. You'd rather be in the Oval Office. Let's have the meeting in there."

That included members of Congress, some of whom had served for years without stepping foot in the Oval Office.

"Go stand behind the desk," he'd tell them. "Sit on the couches. Let's take pictures."

In May 2017, after a ceremony in the Rose Garden celebrating the first step taken to repeal and replace Obamacare, he invited more than seventy members of Congress into the Oval Office. I didn't think everyone could possibly fit in. Yet as he sat behind the desk, members kept piling in, and we took a group photo. The president didn't care that it was crowded. He wanted everyone to join in the victory.

To be honest, he didn't always bring people there just to show off the office. When he was in the Oval, he had the upper hand. He knew it and so did they, and he knew they knew it.

Taking people into the Oval Office, and around the White House in general, was one of the greatest rewards of my job. Cabinet members and staff would often come into the Outer Oval and ask me if they could bring their family or friends to peek into the Oval Office.

"Of course!" I would say if the president wasn't there. I knew he would want as many people as possible to have that opportunity. I loved their reactions when they saw the Oval Office for the first time, often without being told in advance that they were going in.

All of a sudden, there it was, as they had seen it on television for as long as they could remember. Except this was the real deal.

They couldn't believe it. Some cried. Some just stood for the longest time, speechless. How can you not be in awe? For most people, it was a moment they would remember for the rest of their lives. I could relate.

The president often asked his guests, "Shall we go see the residence?"

What was I going to say? "No, Mr. President, you don't have time for that right now"? I wouldn't dare! It meant everything to him.

Off everyone would go for an impromptu tour, which always included the Lincoln Bedroom.

So what if that put him an hour behind schedule? What mattered to him was making his visitors feel at home in, let us not forget, the People's House. President Trump is renting the White House. The American people own it.

If anything, the president was *too* accessible. He had a difficult time saying no.

One afternoon stands out. The president had just learned that several Angel Families, relatives of victims who had been killed by illegal immigrants, were protesting across the street from the White House and wanted to see him. They were upset that the omnibus bill he was about to sign wouldn't have the necessary funds for the much-discussed border wall. He was open to the idea of seeing them.

"They're not on your schedule," everyone argued. "We can't let every group that is protesting something come in to meet with you."

"I don't care," the president said. "Bring them in. I want to talk to them. What they have to say is important."

To Donald Trump, hearing from those people meant much more than sticking to a schedule. He spent more than an hour with them, listening carefully to every story, which were all devastating.

★

Saying no to protect the president's time was my job, and I became good at it. If I hadn't been, there would have been chaos in the Oval Office.

Someone once told me, "You're a traffic cop at the most important intersection in the world."

That was exactly right. People often showed up at my desk or called to ask, "Hey, do you think he wants to see me?" I was always firm, albeit with a gracious smile. "He hasn't asked for you today," I'd say, "so I think we're good for now. But I promise to let you know if that changes." Meanwhile, I was thinking to myself, *The president knows how to find you. If he really wants to see you, he will call for you.*

Anybody who spent too much time with him would not last for long, and the way I figured it, any conversation they would want to have would go a lot better if he were to initiate it.

I knew from experience. I would enter the Oval Office four or five times to interrupt him in a meeting to remind him of another appointment, and he didn't always take it well.

"I got it," he said. "I got it."

On more than a few occasions, when the president was in the dining room, I mentioned I had received a text from Mrs. Trump. She wanted to know where he was and when he would join her in the residence.

"Sir, the first lady is waiting for you," I said.

"Madeleine, I know," he said. "I'll be there when I'm ready."

If it had been anyone else, I would have been content to let him or her wait. But when the first lady called, I made sure he didn't keep her waiting for long. The president was my boss, but the first lady—pardon the pun—trumped everyone.

Once, when a member of the cabinet asked me to reschedule a meeting, which involved several other cabinet secretaries along with staff, I had to move other meetings that had been set up. It was my job to tell the president about such last-minute changes, and I caught some flak for it.

"Why would you do that?" he said. "So now you think it's okay to mess up everyone else's schedule?" He wasn't thinking about himself. He was thinking about everyone else who had to rearrange their day in order to accommodate him.

I wanted to tell him, "Sir, you're the president. Everyone else will adapt to you."

He reacted as anyone else in a stressful job does—and what job is more stressful than being the president of the United States? He would blow off steam every so often at whatever person happened to be nearby. I had to remember it wasn't personal and let it roll off me.

That was easier said than done. There were times on my way home that I called my mom or dad to vent. "The president yelled at me, and it wasn't even my fault," I'd say. "I don't know if I can take this anymore."

Looking back, none of those incidents was nearly as big as I thought at the time. How I wish I was by his side right now. I would vow never to complain again.

You can see why, on some occasions, when the chief of staff or another member of the senior staff told me, "Madeleine, you have got to go back in there and get things moving," referring to the Oval Office, I refused.

"I'm not going back in there," I responded. "I have been in there three times in the last hour. Someone else can go in there. If he sees my face again, he will lose it."

Look, I get it, it's human nature. If you get a chance to spend time with the president in the Oval Office, you're going to take it. To me, however, the people who respected him the most didn't push hard to see him every chance they could. They were mindful of how precious his time truly is.

The cabinet secretaries or members of Congress who waited for the right moment more often than not received a much warmer reception.

"Oh, I haven't heard from Betsy DeVos [the secretary of education] in a while," the president might say after I told him she'd called. "She wants to see me? This must be important. Get her in here." Secretary DeVos, like other members of the cabinet, spoke to the president often, but knew not to take advantage and ask for too many meetings in person.

Unfortunately, others, both in and out of the administration, never stopped pushing. One visitor, whom I won't name, called every time she was in the White House. "If the president wants to see me," she'd say, "I'm here."

Oh, what a coincidence.

What I wanted to tell her, but never actually would, was

"You saw him last week and the week before. Is it really necessary that you see him every time you're here?"

Still, I would have to tell the president that she was in the building—he'd find out eventually—and Donald Trump, being who he is, would respond, "Sure, let her come in."

He would be incredibly gracious, as if he hadn't seen her in years. No wonder she kept calling.

To be fair, she was hardly alone. Quite a few members of Congress phoned to say they just happened to be in the lobby of the West Wing: "If the president wants to see me . . ."

I know, I know.

Again, I didn't have a choice, as that person would undoubtedly tell the president at some point, "I was in the lobby and tried to come see you, but your assistant told me you were busy."

Some were so anxious to see him that they would position themselves in a two-foot space in the Outer Oval where they knew he would be able to see them whenever the door was open. We referred to it as "the line of sight." These people thought they were very clever, but I was onto them.

"Can you move two steps to your right, please?" I would have to say. "If he sees you, he will call you in, his meeting will get interrupted, and we'll be behind schedule."

A number of them would often hang around in the Outer Oval before or after meetings, making a lot of of noise. That was a problem. So, as warmly as I could put it, I would kick them out, and that included four-star generals and foreign diplomats. Sometimes I look back and can't believe the nerve I had.

Even Vice President Pence, for all his noble intentions, would often show up at my desk in the morning to look for him.

"Is the president down yet?" he'd ask.

"No, Mr. Vice President, he's not," I'd say, "but he should be here soon."

"Okay, I'll just pop over to the residence and meet him by the elevator on his way down."

On some occasions, I couldn't figure out why the president didn't simply say, "Mike, I've already seen you five times today."

Every so often, I had no choice but to politely suggest that this might not be a good time. "He's with the lawyers right now," I'd say, "but if you really need to see him, you can go in."

The vice president would take the not-so-subtle hint and say he'd return later. The president is fortunate to have him, and so are the American people. Look no further than the remarkable job he has done as the leader of the Coronavirus Task Force. His calming presence, in contrast to President Trump's high energy, is invaluable.

★

Quite a few, however, who showed up in the Outer Oval refused to accept no for an answer, no matter how strongly I warned them.

"Okay, go in," I'd say, giving up, "but you're walking into the lion's den."

Moments later, they would emerge from the Oval Office with a defeated look on their faces. "You were right," they'd say. "I shouldn't have gone in."

I had a feeling they might listen to me the next time, though many didn't.

I always tried to determine the president's mood, determine when he might need to be alone, and do my best to make sure that happened.

"Who's in there with him?" someone might ask.

"No one," I'd say.

That would really confuse them. "Then why can't I go in?"

"Because he needs ten minutes. Trust me."

The president often gave me tasks when he was in the dining room, but if I didn't hear from him for five or ten minutes, I knew he needed time to read the newspaper, go through some documents, or just take a breath. It was something I couldn't explain. I just felt it. The key to being a valuable assistant is to anticipate the needs of your boss before he knows them himself.

For example, if the staff secretary wanted to present the president with a stack of papers to sign near the end of the day and I knew he wouldn't be thrilled about it, I'd suggest holding off until the following morning, unless it was urgent.

Not surprisingly, being strict about who the president could see and when he could see them didn't earn me the title of Miss Congeniality.

*So what?* I thought at the time. To do my job, I had to get to the point where I wasn't worried what people thought of me. All they needed to know was: You are not going into the Oval Office, period.

For other staffers, their main focus was on policy or messaging. Sure, they cared about the president, but whenever it came to putting something on his plate or giving him a break, they didn't hesitate to bother him.

Not me. Not ever.

Donald Trump, you see, was not just my main focus; he was my only focus. That wasn't true about anyone else in the West Wing: Stephen Miller, a senior policy advisor, Kellyanne, Jared, or any of the three chiefs of staff while I was there. Each person had a specific portfolio to focus on.

What I found most disrespectful was when people walked into and out of the Oval Office during meetings or showed up late. Are you kidding me? What could possibly be more important than a meeting with the president?

I thought it was incredibly rude when staff members asked me to pass notes to their bosses who were in meetings in the Oval Office. People, this isn't high school!

The president, though, didn't seem to mind, so I began to use it to my advantage, taking my own notes in to him when he needed to wrap up a meeting or when he was in the dining room with the vice president in the evening. At times the VP kept POTUS [president of the United States] longer than we hoped. He needed to call it a day, as did the rest of us.

To move things along, I would bring in a note given to me by the VP's aide: "Mr. Vice President, the second lady is wondering when you're going to be home for dinner."

The boss would seize the opportunity: "Mike, go, have a good night."

Did the president know how much I guarded his time? Probably not. He couldn't see it when people were *not* coming in. Yet no doubt he recognized when it was five o'clock and he hadn't enjoyed a second of downtime in hours.

How, you may wonder, did this supposedly self-conscious young woman get up the nerve to essentially order the most powerful people in Washington to keep their distance from the president?

It became easy, to be honest. I had a job to do. I can be self-conscious and anxious when I don't have any control over the situation. Those closed-door meetings with Stephanie and Hogan after the dinner in Bedminster come to mind.

Yet when it was on my terms—when I was greeter girl is another example—I felt emboldened to tell anyone to do anything, and you know what, I actually enjoyed it. That doesn't mean I'm proud of the way I went about it, sometimes.

Over time, I also became aware of, depending on his mood, which person might be the best for the president to see and did whatever was necessary to arrange it. One day, it might be Sarah Sanders; another, Hope Hicks, Dan Scavino, or maybe Stephen Miller. It was not always easy to know. Sarah was the one I turned to if the president was upset about a story in the press. "You need to get in here," I'd tell her. "You need to tell him that this is fake news."

On occasion, getting her to agree took some serious arm-twisting. "Are you sure? I really don't want to go in there," she would tell me. "Please don't make me."

"I know you don't," I'd say, "but he needs you."

Sarah adored the president; it wasn't that. But like me, she knew there were only so many times he would be happy to see her on any given day.

A lot of times, what he needed was to talk to somebody who didn't care that he is the president, who loves him for who he is. His family, for example.

Not long ago, I found this entry in one of the two journals I still have: "The President often calls his family just to say hello. . . . It is so nice to see a different side of him—the genuine, more personal side. Very refreshing."

One time, Gianni Infantino, the president of FIFA, the soccer federation, came to the White House.

Barron is a huge soccer fan, so the president told me to let his son know that Mr. Infantino was in the Oval Office. Barron met him and they posed for some pictures. I was struck by how thoughtful the gesture was. The president, in the middle of a busy workday, was taking the time to give his son a memory he would always cherish.

I was moved, as well, by the sweet way he spoke to the first lady. "Hi, honey, I'll be home in about fifteen minutes," I often heard him tell Mrs. Trump. "Love you."

Whenever he returned from a trip, even if it was just to attend an event in town, the president would ask me to place a call to her before he went back to work. "Just wanted to let you know I'm here," he'd say. "Yes, it was very successful. See you later."

It occurred to me that beyond the trappings of power, the president and Mrs. Trump are just another married couple. I witnessed the tremendous affection and respect they have for each other, and it's clear that they have figured out a way to make their relationship thrive. It's remarkable given the pressures they face.

I also told him right away whenever I heard from one of his sisters or his brother. They always understood if he was busy. "Just give Donald my love," they would say. "I don't need to talk to him." That meant the world to the president, and he'd always call them back.

There were, of course, the usual self-serving calls and requests: "Can you get me into an event?" "Can you put in a good word for me?" I suppose it was no different with anyone else who has occupied that office.

"I haven't heard from that person in ten years," the president would say, "and now he wants to come see me?"

On occasion, without any agenda, I connected the president with Robert Kraft, the owner of the New England Patriots. It would be refreshing for him to have a conversation with a true friend, someone, for a change, who didn't want something from him. Just about everyone else did.

That wasn't the case with Bob Kraft. He and the president have been close friends for years. The two just wanted to catch up.

Two or three times a year, when I thought he hadn't had a fun night in a while, I arranged for a group of his New York buddies to pay him a visit. It was just a bunch of guys getting together, and he loved it. We never knew what tomorrow would bring, but for one evening, at least, he had a reprieve from the rigors of the day.

There were also occasions, often near the end of the day, when Dan, who has been with Donald Trump since long before he entered politics, would go into the dining room and sit with the president, just to keep him company.

Many times, Dan stepped out for a minute and walked over to my desk. "It's your turn, Maddie," he said. "Come in and and sit with us."

Looking back, those moments were among my favorites. The three of us sat there and reflected on the day.

Dan had his finger on the pulse of the base, constantly scanning social media for videos or memes made by supporters. After the Mueller Report came out, there were outrageous stories claiming that Donald Trump was looking into the idea of altering the Twenty-second Amendment, which limits a president to two terms. Dan discovered a video that we showed the president immediately. It featured yard signs with TRUMP 2024 . . . TRUMP 2072 . . . TRUMP 8000 . . . and finally TRUMP 4EVA.

The president loved it. "Put it out," he said.

We did just that, and the haters, as we expected, went crazy. God forbid that Donald Trump have a sense of humor.

Speaking of Robert Mueller, Dan and I once showed the president a spoof video of the former FBI director. That was right after Mueller testified on the Hill. I had never seen the president laugh so hard. He was almost in tears. This is great, we thought. He certainly needs some comic relief after everything he went through with the Russia investigation.

Dan and I were a tag team. No wonder it pains me so greatly when I think about what happened to our friendship after I left the White House. I called him the day I apologized to the president. He was distant as never before, and we haven't spoken since.

"Madeleine, it is very hard for me right now, knowing you did this," he said.

★

When I think back to those who took advantage of the president's time, I can't help but think of Lindsey Graham and one night in particular.

I was at the Hamilton, a restaurant in DC, with Ben and his sister when I received a call from Senator Graham around seven. He was in a car with Nebraska senator Ben Sasse and Texas senator Ted Cruz.

"We're on our way to the White House," Lindsey said.

"You mean right now?" I asked.

"Yes, right now. We're about five minutes away."

"Does the president know you're coming?"

"No, but we really need to see him."

Gee, I hadn't heard that one before. As always, I knew I had to call the president to let him know.

"Do you want to see them, or would you like me to say you're not available?" I asked.

I could tell he wasn't excited about the idea. Who could blame him? He was in for the night, having dinner with the first lady and Barron. Whatever the senators wanted, couldn't it wait until the morning?

Apparently not.

Nonetheless, as usual, President Trump wasn't about to say no. "Okay, let them come," he said, "but tell them it needs to be quick."

I left the Hamilton right away and literally ran the two blocks to the White House. Somebody had to clear them for entry. You can't simply show up at the gate and walk in. This is the White House, not the Waffle House.

I was polite when the senators arrived, but I wanted them to know that they were infringing on the president's personal time. "Let me walk you up," I suggested. "The president was having dinner with his family, but he'll see you anyway."

They did appear a bit sorry but obviously not sorry enough to cancel their visit. As for it being a "quick" meeting, they hung out in the residence for about an hour, enjoying hors d'oeuvres.

It's amazing, though, how much energy the president has for a man his age. For any age. Some evenings, when he was still busy in the Oval Office, we'd all look at each other, wondering "Oh, God, how do we get him out of here?" Once he went to the residence, we could take off, as well. Not a minute before.

If there was no note from someone's staffer I could take him, I would have to resort to Plan B. "Sir, West Wing tours are starting in ten minutes," I'd say. "Do you want us to postpone them?"

The tours started at about 8:30 p.m. but would have to be delayed or even canceled if he was working late.

"No, I'll go up," he'd say. "Have a good night, kids."

Still, I'm not suggesting that the gravity of his responsibility never wore on him. Of course it did. He's human and has a job in which others have been known to not age very gracefully.

The subject of his energy level, however, was taboo in the West Wing.

"He looks exhausted," I once told Hope early on.

She set me straight right away. "Donald Trump is never tired," she said, "and he is never sick."

Got it. I never mentioned it again.

# CHAPTER ELEVEN

# *Reconnecting the Old-Fashioned Way*

I was extremely proud of where I worked and the person I worked for, and it wouldn't have mattered how much money another employer might have offered me to leave my position. Nothing could possibly have been more gratifying than being in the White House and spending every day with the president.

That's what worries me sometimes. I'm not even thirty years old, and I might already have had the best job I'll ever have. Where do I possibly go from here?

That doesn't mean, however, that I told everyone I happened to come across that I worked for President Trump. Quite the opposite. I carefully read the room first to make sure they wouldn't attack me.

The people who despise Donald Trump are everywhere, and they're not shy about telling you exactly how they feel. If anything, they go out of their way to express themselves.

Most times, if they attacked the president, I didn't take the bait. What would that achieve? Anyone who has that much hate in his heart won't listen to reason.

What amazed me was that, since I am a young woman, they presumed that I felt the same way. They didn't bother to ask. That proves how arrogant—and ignorant—they are. And I thought people were close-minded when I worked on the Romney campaign. "How can you be a Republican?" they'd asked me all the time. The nerve of me.

Multiply that by a thousand when it comes to Donald Trump. I was at a friend's bachelorette party last year when some of the girls asked the most innocent questions about the White House, nothing to do with politics or the individuals who live there. Even that was too much for some.

"I can't listen to this conversation," remarked one girl, who abruptly left the room.

I didn't say a word to her in the president's defense.

Looking back, I have asked myself: Should I have stood up for the president that day and other times when someone criticized him? Is that what he would have expected me to do?

Maybe, but, honestly, most of the time, I was afraid of how the other person might react. People have become so hostile to any opposing point of view. That's what we've come to in this country. No wonder the polls do not accurately reflect the amount of support there is for President Trump. Many don't want to invite the abuse.

There were a number of occasions, though, when I did speak out. There was only so much I could take.

"Donald Trump hates immigrants, and he's racist," someone once told me.

"That's not true at all," I responded. "The president is very pro-immigration, but the people coming into our country need to respect our laws and come in legally. He encourages immigration. His wife is an immigrant."

On a few occasions while I was in a taxi, the driver would be listening to the radio and blurt out, "This president is terrible."

I would fire back, "He's doing a great job, actually. I love him!"

That would pretty much end the conversation.

For the most part, though, I was ashamed that I had to maintain a low profile, being as proud as I was of what President Trump is doing for this country. The staff who worked for Obama didn't have to hide their feelings. They could have put a bumper sticker on their foreheads and marched down Pennsylvania Avenue, and people would have applauded them.

I reminded myself, however, that I was taking a stand every day by showing up in the Outer Oval, prepared to do whatever the president asked.

Fortunately, most of the people I spent my time with supported him, though they registered one recurring complaint.

"Oh, my gosh, I love the president, I really do," they said, "and I love what he's been doing for the American people, but, for God's sake, he has to stop tweeting. You're with him all the time. Is there anything you can do to get him to stop?"

Sure thing. I will march into the Oval Office first thing tomorrow and tell him he has to stop tweeting. He'll thank me and wonder why he didn't think of the idea himself.

Seriously, no one, myself included, would ever dare tell the president to stop doing something that brought him so much pleasure and, in my opinion, provided such an important service.

Have you lost it, Madeleine? Hold on, let me explain.

For the first time, we have a president—no matter how you feel about his message and tone—who tells us, hour by hour, what he thinks. It's akin to someone keeping a diary, except it's a diary that everyone has a chance to read.

The fact that the president does *not* edit his thoughts is quite refreshing, and what he tweets is infinitely more revealing than the choreographed press conferences his predecessors staged. Think about it: Can you recall one compelling comment Barack Obama or George W. Bush made in those forums? I assume most presidents just hope to get out of there without making any major gaffes.

The choice, as Stephanie Grisham, the former press secretary, put it to the media was, in essence: Would you rather have me in the briefing room for forty-five minutes three times a week or the president all day, every day?

Case closed.

What cracked me up were the members of Congress who wanted him to stop tweeting but then encouraged him to put something out when it served their purposes, whether it was a bill they had sponsored or they were seeking an endorsement for an upcoming election.

Exhibits A and B: Mitch McConnell and Paul Ryan, the former speaker of the House. On numerous occasions, Ryan asked the president to show support for a Republican running for Congress. The president was happy to oblige. "*Now* you love my tweets," he joked.

So, too, by the way, do the media. They would never admit it, given the state of war they declared from day one, but the more controversial the president is, the better their ratings, and nothing means more to them than ratings.

Needless to say, that reality didn't escape him. The TV set near my desk had four quadrants on at the same time, tuned to Fox, Fox Business, CNN, and MSNBC.

When he stopped in the Outer Oval and took a quick glance, each of the screens, many times, showed him in one context or another. "All Trump, all the time," he'd remark.

Early in his term, he had a television put into the private dining room off the Oval Office, where he spent a good chunk of time reading the newspapers, working quietly, and catching up on old correspondence.

The dining room became his working office, while the Oval was kept pristine and ceremonial. Stacks and stacks of papers covered almost every inch of the room. It was a mess, but it was an organized mess. He knew exactly what was in each stack.

Obama, from what I was told, spent more time in the study off the Oval Office, which President Trump referred to as "the Monica Room." I don't have to say anything more.

In the beginning, we used that room as a storage closet. As time went on, I realized that it would be an excellent place to store gifts. The president loves to give gifts to his visitors, such as lapel pins, water bottles, candles, watches, golf balls, cuff links, and decoupage boxes depicting the White House. His favorite was a beautiful silver tray with the presidential seal.

The president wrote a lot of tweets from the dining room. That's not saying much. He tweeted from everywhere. He used to say that if he were to stop, Twitter would go broke. That's an exaggeration, no doubt, but you get the point.

How did this tweeting thing work in the White House, anyway?

For starters, when I was there, only two people had access to the account and could hit "Send": Presidnt Trump and Dan Scavino. Most of the tweets, especially in the odd, nonworking hours came from the president, often without him giving anybody a chance to weigh in. I suppose that was the point.

Did that make some folks in the West Wing a little nervous? You bet it did, particularly on weekends, when the president didn't have much scheduled. The concern was that he would see a story on Fox or a conspiracy theory on Twitter and feel the need to weigh in.

A single tweet, in an instant, can change the whole narrative planned for the day. Forget about infrastructure or the new tax bill; today is going to be about North Korea.

On several occasions, people somehow found out what the president was going to tweet, and soon there were about a dozen people crammed outside the Oval Office, everyone wanting to offer their opinion. They were in his line of sight, the message being "You can't put that out!"

I heard people in the West Wing complain on a regular basis, "I wish he had thought this out a little more" or "If only I could have told him what I thought before he tweeted."

I have news for them: in almost every case, it wouldn't have made a difference. As he pointed out whenever people pushed back, "I'm the president. It's my decision."

Once, Steven Mnuchin, the Treasury secretary, became so anxious about a tweet the president was working on that he brought me into it. The tweet, he said, was inaccurate and could possibly undo a lot of important work his staff had recently accomplished. "This can't go out the way it is," he said. "Call me before this goes out so I can speak to the president."

No problem. I always tried to accommodate members of the cabinet the best I could.

Only the day quickly got out of hand, as many did, and I forgot about the tweet. Lo and behold, the tweet, without the secretary conferring with the president, went out at 8:15 p.m.:

> I am not a fan of Bitcoin and other Cryptocurrencies, which are not money, and whose value is highly volatile and based on thin air. Unregulated Crypto Assets can facilitate unlawful behavior, including drug trade and other illegal activity....

Secretary Mnuchin was not pleased. He called me at home roughly an hour later. "I told you to tell me," he said. I apologized, explaining it was an honest mistake.

You might not believe this, but most of the time, the president does not set out to write harmful tweets. Even when he is attacking someone, he is often cracking himself, and his aides, up over a new nickname he's thought of. I especially liked "Pocahontas" in reference to Senator Warren, and "Sleepy Joe Biden."

Seriously, I know his tweets can be harsh, but try to remember how maligned the president is by the media, day after day. The tweets are his way of fighting back by going around the reporters and speaking directly to the people. Without the tweets, the press would have even more power to dictate the agenda.

"Should I tweet this?" the president frequently asked Dan and me.

"Go ahead," we'd respond, with very few exceptions. "It's so savage, but let's do it!"

The way we saw it, the liberals were going to hate Donald Trump no matter what he did, so he might as well give it right back to them. We would always say to one another, "He's the president, and she's not." I think you know who "she" is.

I'm not suggesting, by the way, that I was in favor of every tweet he put out. Give me a little more credit than that. More than a few definitely crossed the line, especially those that referred to a woman's appearance.

If he ran any by me that I didn't particularly like before they went out, I didn't hesitate to offer my opinion. In no way was I attempting to stop the president from tweeting, only questioning if the tweet was appropriate. We stopped a few, which was probably for the better. One that comes to mind was a harsh tweet about Nancy Pelosi—about her health, I seem to recall. The line between funny and mean is a very thin one, especially when you sit with the president and know the kind of mood he might be in. One misplaced word can make a huge difference.

Now, I can almost hear what you're thinking: What about the tweets that contain foul language? How are we supposed to tell our kids that it's wrong to use such words when the leader of our country uses them?

I can't offer excuses, only an explanation. Again, it's the price we must pay for his being authentic, which I far prefer to another president who runs every word by his staff. It's similar to the studios in Hollywood that show a new film to focus groups before they release it to the general public and then pick the ending the audience likes the most.

Besides, the American people knew about his tweets long before the election and still voted for him. It's not as if he underwent a sudden personality change the moment he took office.

The tweets he didn't write himself, he dictated to Dan, myself, or another staffer. We typed them up and brought them back to President Trump for review.

The president usually made some minor edits, and we then showed him the revised version. This could go on four or five times until the tweet was ready to go.

Some, if they featured intricate policy details, were likely crafted by an official from one of the agencies or a member of the speechwriting team. The president would then have to issue his approval. Not one tweet was posted unless he signed off on it.

Dan Scavino, who now serves as the White House deputy chief of staff for communications, was the ideal person for this role. The two go back to the early 1990s, when Dan caddied for him at Briar Hall Country Club, which became Trump National Golf Club Westchester. Dan later became the club's general manager.

He wasn't a policy guy, but that didn't matter. He fulfilled a role that was just as vital, seeming to always know what the president was thinking and what he needed. Dan served as the bridge between Donald Trump's old life and new life. The two loved to reminisce about the good old days.

★

As much as the president loved to tweet, he wasn't into technology the way Obama was. The only times I saw him on a laptop were when the staff wanted to show him something online.

He even resisted when we tried to get him to use an iPad to look over the hundreds of photos that the White House photographer took every week. No chance. The president had to see the actual prints. He's as old school as you can get.

Often, when I found him in the dining room reading the newspaper, I couldn't bring myself to go in. He seemed so much at peace. The people who suggest that the president doesn't read don't know what they are talking about. He reads constantly.

So forget about the tweets. The telephone is his preferred means of communication by far. I set up more calls for the president and received more calls than I could ever count. They took up a large portion of my day.

Even when I went to get coffee in the Navy Mess, located in the basement, I took my cell phone, to which calls to my office line were transferred. To be gone from the Outer Oval Office for more than two minutes felt like two weeks. I practically sprinted through the West Wing most days—in four-inch heels, I might add.

There wasn't much of a respite on evenings or weekends, either.

"Oh, my goodness," a caller would say when I answered on a Sunday morning. "What are you doing in the office on the weekend?"

"You know me, just working all the time," I'd say.

I was joking, though it certainly felt as though I was. I couldn't afford not to answer the phone. What if the one call I missed turned out to be the most important of the day?

Sure, that kind of schedule has a tendency to interfere with your personal life, but, again, the White House was my life, and I was serving a president who relied on the telephone 24/7. Besides, I'd figured out pretty quickly what I was in for in this job. I was fortunate to have Ben, who knew the political world quite well. He didn't mind when I had to pause a movie for the fifth time to take a call.

Some people reached out more than others, such as Jared, who tracked me down on many a Sunday afternoon with a favor to ask: "Can you call the president and ask if he'll do this tomorrow?"

I'd think to myself, *I don't want to call him on the weekend, the only time he gets a break. He sees me every day.*

Of course, Jared didn't want to bug him, either, so I would make the call.

That doesn't mean I let him know about everyone who called in to the White House operator. That would have been insane. The operators receive thousands of calls per day.

Here's how it worked: Unless you had my direct line, you would call the White House switchboard and an operator would answer. You would give them your name and ask for the president. If you were one of the approved callers—the president's family, the members of the cabinet, the senior staff, his personal friends—you'd be patched through to me without delay. As you can tell, to be an approved caller is a big deal.

The names of those who qualified were kept on an electronic file, which Molly, who took over for me, now has, along with the operators and the chief of staff's office. The names are constantly updated. For example, suppose you are forced to leave the administration. Before you can say "Rex Tillerson," you're no longer an approved caller.

Hmm, I wonder how quickly they took my name off.

The Chief of Staff's office and I removed and added names all the time, such as Kevin McCarthy, who became the House Minority Leader in 2018, and other members of Congress who called practically every day. That way, I didn't have to approve them whenever they called.

If a name wasn't in the file but the operators confirmed that it was a well-known individual, they still transferred the call to me. If they couldn't verify the person's identity or thought it was probably a prank, they would say that the president wasn't available. If they weren't sure, the operator would check with me first: "There is a John Smith on the phone, and he says he has known the president for twenty years. Do you know this person?"

"Yeah, put him through" or "Send him to my voice mail," I'd say if the name was familiar.

If it wasn't, I told the operator it likely wasn't a legitimate caller. I pretty much knew everyone who might try to reach the president, but I checked with other staff members, the first family, and even the internet when I wasn't sure.

People were shocked at how fast I put them through, and it didn't have to be someone as powerful as Rupert Murdoch.

"I just want to leave a message for the president," they would say.

"No need to leave a message," I said. "I've got him right now."

"You do? Really?"

Then, if the president was sitting in the Oval Office with the door open, I would transfer the call to his phone and shout, for example, "That's Mitch!" I always found it odd to be shouting to the president of the United States, but we had a system of communication that worked perfectly for us.

Every so often, a freshman congressman would call and I would put him on the president's missed calls list.

"Who is this?" he'd ask. "I don't recognize this name."

After I told him, he would almost always say, "Okay, call him." I'm telling you, the man called everyone back.

Some mornings when I got up, I'd have twenty emails from the operator. That was how many calls the president had already been on and it was not even eight o'clock. Every time he called somebody, I received an email, as did the chief of staff, his military aides, and others in the Outer Oval.

Later that morning when the president arrived in the Oval Office, he would ask for any additional calls.

"Mr. President, I don't have any calls for you," I'd say.

No calls? You've got to be kidding. At Trump Tower, he used to tell me, he had received hundreds of calls every day.

"Now I'm the president of the United States and no one has called me? That doesn't make sense."

Yes, it did, though I never told him that. The staff took a lot of calls on his behalf.

People got frustrated with me at times when I put callers directly through without coordinating with the proper office. Still, I knew the president wouldn't be very happy if he found out someone he wanted to talk with hadn't been able to reach him.

★

President Trump has such a distinctive voice, I think it intimidates a lot of people. It intimidated me, that's for sure. No matter how many times I spoke to him, whenever the operator came on and said, "The president is on the phone for you," my stomach dropped.

Why is he calling me? What did I do now?

There was nothing to worry about. Most of the time, he was calling to ask when his first meeting of the day was or if I'd set something up he was waiting to hear about.

Speaking of calls the president made, it's impossible not to mention the one that has received the most scrutiny, on July 25, 2019, with the Ukrainian president, Volodymyr Zelensky.

I was sitting on my couch at home last September when the news broke—I had left the White House not long before—and it reminded me of how difficult it could be to connect him with foreign leaders.

"Call Macron," the president would often shout at me from the Oval Office, or "Get me Justin," referring to Emmanuel Macron, the president of France and Justin Trudeau, the prime minister of Canada.

I sometimes got the feeling he thought it was as easy as ordering a pizza. No, siree.

First, I'd have to notify the White House Situation Room, which would then put in a formal request, through the National Security Council, to the staff responsible for that country. From there it would go to the country's embassy in DC and finally to the leader's office.

At the same time, we had to track down translators when necessary and anyone in Washington or abroad who needed to listen in on the call.

That could take hours. Meanwhile, President Trump was sitting in the Oval Office, wondering: Am I ever going to get this person on the phone?

He would—eventually.

Lots of times, however, when I placed a call for the president within the United States, there would be a delay as well, although it would have nothing to do with protocol. The exchanges could be very amusing.

"Hi, this is Madeleine, I have the president on the phone for your boss."

"The president of what?"

"The president of the United States! I promise this isn't a prank. Put your boss on the phone, please. President Trump is waiting."

Whoever it was, once the person heard the president's voice, it was over. That's how powerful he is on the phone, and the power doesn't relate just to the office itself. It comes from the conviction he has in every conversation, regardless of what the subject might be. I have never met anyone so engaged in every moment of life.

The power also comes from his former life as a businessman. He used the phone to make deals, to build his fortune, to be Donald Trump.

Old school.

★

# CHAPTER TWELVE

# The Perks and Perils of Power

With each passing day, I not only felt more comfortable in the West Wing, I felt more powerful. I realize now that wasn't necessarily a good thing. It led to my making decisions, sometimes unconsciously, so I would not have to give up any of that power. That's how intoxicating power can be.

Believe me, I was far from alone. Everybody in that building, at one point or another, does something to hold on to power if not consolidate it. If you don't, you tell yourself, you will fall behind and might never catch up.

Just like with the greeter girl, I didn't devise some master plan for how I could become powerful in the West Wing. I was happy simply doing my job. Yet as time went on and I watched everyone else become obsessed with their titles and ranks and salaries, it became difficult not to care just as much.

For me, it first manifested itself in the way I dealt with the two people most responsible for my being in the White House, Katie Walsh and Reince Priebus. They deserved better, and three years later, I still feel ashamed I wasn't as loyal to them as I could have been.

When I met Katie in the summer of 2013, I couldn't have been more impressed. She is only six years older than I am, but she was much more mature, and for someone who had yet to turn thirty, she was incredibly accomplished. I looked up to her and told myself, this is the person I want to be in five years.

She didn't have it easy in the beginning of her career. As a young, attractive blond woman, Katie wasn't taken seriously by the men she worked with. Imagine that. Yet she didn't complain one bit, which was the right way to respond. Making it an issue wouldn't have done her any good.

Instead, she focused on the task ahead. The harder she worked and the more she asserted herself, the more the men noticed her intelligence and not just her good looks. She was like a big sister to me, somebody I could always call on when I had problems at work or in my social life. She helped me see the path forward.

Unfortunately, when Katie arrived in the West Wing, the deputy chief of staff job wasn't what she had anticipated. She'd been the chief of staff for the Republican National Committee during a presidential election and had done as much as anybody, except maybe for Reince, to help the party regain the White House and do as well as it did in the House and Senate races. Besides mastering the details, she always saw the big picture. Take the emphasis she placed on accumulating data and building infrastructure.

The big picture was also what she had planned to focus on in the White House. Only there was no time for that, not with the twenty-four-hour news cycle and a president who constantly changed the topic of conversation. Instead she oversaw the president's schedule, and that was a no-win position. The staff complained that she didn't schedule enough meetings. Everyone felt that his or her agenda was the most important. At the same time, the president complained that his schedule was becoming unbearable. He had a point; everyone was seeking time with him.

Worse yet, Katie was caught in the power struggle among Reince, Jared, and Steve Bannon that plagued the early months of the Trump White House. Looking back, it was so unnecessary. It was difficult enough trying to run a new administration.

In March of 2017, when she was a victim of that struggle, she resigned, and the press was all over it.

I felt awful for her, but I stayed as far away from the controversy as possible. I could claim I was too busy trying to learn the nuances of my own job, but it would be a lie. I didn't want to get caught up in what would be the first of numerous stories about White House palace intrigue.

About six months later, I was a bridesmaid in her wedding, but after that, we grew apart. I felt I had no choice but to distance myself from her and anyone else who was still considered by the Trump loyalists to be an "RNC person." If I'd continued to be close to her, I might not have gained the trust of the president and his family. That was something I was not willing to risk.

I made the decision early on that I would hitch myself to the person who sat behind the Resolute Desk over everyone else. That's why I guarded his time so fiercely and didn't care whom that might offend.

After Katie left, there was one less person I had to be loyal to, and it meant I was one step closer to the president. I was around him all day, every day, and it occurred to me that maybe

I didn't need anybody else. Better yet, everyone else needed me. I was the gatekeeper.

Besides, the closer you are to the president, the more likely you'll be invited to enjoy the perks that came with the power of his office, such as riding on Air Force One and Marine One.

Nothing, however, matched the trips to Camp David. I think about them a lot.

Getting there isn't easy unless you're lucky enough to fly on Marine One with POTUS. The White House provides you with directions, but there is no big sign at the side of the road that says "Camp David next exit." Miss the turn, and you could very well find yourself lost in the Catoctin mountains.

Once you arrive, you have to hand in any personal cell phones, laptops, and iPads. Believe me, it's worth it. You're only seventy miles from DC, but it might as well be seventy *million* miles.

Camp David, formally Naval Support Facility Thurmont, is just that, a camp, with a swimming pool, basketball courts, tennis courts, bowling alley, arcade room, workout facility, skeet shooting, movie theater—basically, any activity you might desire. A group of us went skeet shooting once with the marines. I wore a vest, earphones, and goggles—the works. It was thrilling, although once was enough for me.

Camp David also offers something even more enriching: peace, a chance to reflect, away from the chaos and controversy Washington feeds on.

No wonder every president since Eisenhower has loved it. The press isn't there. That in itself makes it paradise. It's the only place in the world the president can go without any advance planning.

The camp's staff, which consists of officers and enlisted servicemen and women in the navy and marine corps, worried that it might not compare favorably to his more luxurious homes, renovated the property soon after President Trump took office. The cabins are beautiful, as if they came out of a Restoration Hardware catalog.

The best part, though, is that the president treats Camp David the same as he treats Air Force One: he shares it with everyone. When it's movie night, he invites every member of the camp staff and their families. He did that a lot of times in the White House, as well.

"Invite the people," he would tell me.

I was never quite sure whom he meant by "the people," so it was up to me to figure it out. I invited those from as many groups as possible. One night, it would be members of the advance team; another, a group from the Secret Service or the White House Military Office. I tried to focus on those who had never been offered such perks.

For the president, the downtime was essential. It was similar to the rejuvenation he enjoyed when he went to his club in Virginia to play golf. He gets a lot of criticism for golfing too much, but Obama and many other former presidents played just as often. Of course, the press adored Obama, so he got a pass. Now, having worked in the White House, I understand why presidents get out of the office whenever they have the chance.

Even when President Trump went to the course or Camp David, he was still working, answering every call that came in.

★

Another big thrill for me was to ride in the Beast.

That's the nickname for the car the president rides in. It was first called that during George W. Bush presidency. You don't just jump in, oh no. You have to be invited by the boss himself.

I was in the Oval Office when I told him he'd better hurry if he was going to make it in time for a lunch with Senate Republicans on the Hill. He got up, and, as he was walking out the door, pointed to everyone in the room—myself, Hogan Gidley, and Pat Cipollone. "You guys want to come? You want to see how Congress works?"

Did we ever! Except in my case, I paused for a moment, wondering if members of the staff would ask one another: Why is Madeleine riding in the Beast? I knew that taking advantage of opportunities like this didn't come without upsetting someone. You have to ask yourself: Is it worth it?

The Beast? Absolutely. This could very well be my only chance, and it was.

I soon found myself sitting directly across from the president, my back to the driver. I couldn't believe my good fortune, and you know what, I wasn't the only one to revel in the moment.

"How cool is this?" the president said.

He then tapped on the glass. "Feel how thick this is," he said. "It's bulletproof."

Next came the perfect Donald Trump exchange with Tony, the head of his Secret Service detail.

"Tony," the president joked, "these people are probably not high enough to be allowed in the Beast, are they?"

"No, sir," Tony, stone-faced, said, "they're not."

"But it's okay, because I invited them."

"Yes, sir, you can do whatever you want."

The ride was over in five minutes, maybe less, but I could now take the Beast off my White House bucket list.

The president is always trying to share these once-in-a-lifetime experiences with others. Say he's headed to Florida for a political rally. At the last minute, he will invite a dozen senators along. Somebody from the advance team or the Secret Service has to then give him the news: "Sir, there simply aren't enough seats on the plane for you to take everyone."

If you think that answer would suffice, you don't know Donald Trump.

"Tell them to sit in my cabin," he would respond.

"Unfortunately, we can't do that. The TSA won't let us. Only a certain number of people can legally be on the plane."

So out go the nonessential staff who were manifested for that trip, and in go the senators. The president usually finds a way to get what he wants.

For me, however, it wasn't only the perks I received; it was the praise. I couldn't get enough. It goes back again to my inherent need for approval.

Every time a cabinet secretary or a member of the senior staff brought someone into the Outer Oval Office, they would stop at my desk. I heard all the time: "This is Madeleine, the most important person in the West Wing. She's the one who makes things run around here. We all answer to her." I knew they were humoring me, but I loved it. Who wouldn't?

On occasion, I received word from Sean Hannity or someone else close to the president, something to the effect of "He told me what a great job you're doing."

I can't overstate how awesome I felt whenever someone told me that. In the White House, you are never given an official job performance review.

The power. The perks. The praise. No wonder I was convinced that the president would never fire me.

I was invincible.

★

Even after I distanced myself from Katie, some people in the building still regarded me as her "spy," up to the day I was forced out as a matter of fact. That's how deeply they mistrusted anybody who had not been with President Trump from the beginning. I felt as though I had to constantly defend my past life.

"You wanted Marco, you didn't want us here" I heard over and over. "You're an RNC person."

My standard response: "I'm not an RNC person. I'm a Trump person." Frankly, by that point, I saw no difference.

Not that I would have been fired if someone from the White House had, for example, seen Katie and me having lunch one day. It doesn't work that way. How they responded would be much more subtle. I would have stopped being invited to meetings or no longer been kept in the loop on various matters. I saw that years later with certain members of the staff. The president has some forceful advocates on his behalf, but not everybody in the West Wing trusts everybody else. That's human nature, I suppose, and I'm certain it's like that in every administration.

When Jared invited me to sit in on the Monday meetings related to the 2020 election, he listed one condition: that I wouldn't share anything with a specific staff member, who was suspected throughout the building of being a leaker.

Why, if that were the case, did the president keep the person around? Because, remember, he doesn't like to confront people or hurt their feelings. President Trump didn't tell me I had to leave the White House. Mick did.

Yes, I know, the comments the president makes often hurt people's feelings, but that's because he has no other option. The media and the Democrats, even Hollywood, blame him for everything. If he were treated with respect or even given the benefit of the doubt, he wouldn't be anywhere near as combative. Just imagine if it were you who was being attacked all the time.

"My comms [communications] team doesn't fight for me," he used to say, "so I have to do it myself."

As, for example, when the president decided, in late 2018, to ban Jim Acosta, the biased CNN reporter, from the White House. Everyone told him he couldn't do it.

"I don't care," he said. "I want him out."

His press pass would ultimately be reinstated, but that wasn't the point. The president won't back down when the press is unfair to him, and his base loves him for it.

Another reason he keeps leakers or troublemakers around is that he prefers to have them on the inside rather than on the outside, where they might cause a lot more damage. He has enough critics.

On occasion, however, to his detriment, he kept people around much longer than he probably should have.

The best, or worst, example was his former aide Omarosa Manigault Newman, director of communications for the Office of Public Liaison. She sat in on meetings that she had no business being in just because she said she needed to represent the African American community.

Omarosa felt entitled, and for no good reason. One story tells all you need to know. She was hoping to have her wedding in the White House and assumed that no one would object. She assumed wrong.

Lindsay Reynolds, then the first lady's chief of staff, shut the idea down in a hurry. No one is allowed to get married in the White House unless he or she is a member of the family. Mrs. Trump doesn't approve of the staff using the residence for personal reasons. Though the White House may be the People's House, the private residence is just that, a private residence.

Instead, Omarosa had her wedding at the Trump Hotel, but—get this—wearing her wedding dress, she took her entire bridal party to the gate of the White House the same day to take some photos. She caused quite a scene, and the Secret Service had to physically prevent her from entering. How embarrassing to have that happen on your wedding day!

I was thrilled when General Kelly, then chief of staff, forced her out near the end of 2017 and the president saw Omarosa for who she was, someone who cared only about herself. Even so, I was upset that the general had allowed her to clear out her office and make a graceful exit.

★

Once I left the White House, Katie and I talked a lot, making up for lost time. It was almost as though the last two years had never happened. We had dinner at her house in Virginia shortly after I came back from California.

I was grateful she didn't hold my behavior against me. I doubt whether I would have shown as much character.

Katie told me how deeply it had hurt to have her name dragged through the mud by the media after she resigned. There were days she couldn't get out of bed. Tell me about it.

However, even after Katie left, I was still seen as "a Reince person."

For how much longer that perception would last, that was unclear.

One of the reasons Reince put me into the Outer Oval Office was to keep an eye on things for him: Who is the president meeting with? Who is he calling? Who is calling him?

The chief of staff's office is maybe fifty feet from the Oval Office. That doesn't seem far, but a lot can go on without his ever knowing it.

Which put me into a very awkward position. Whom was my allegiance to? To Reince, the man who had brought me in? Or to the president, the man I was growing closer to every day?

I think you know whom I chose.

As you might expect, that caused tension between Reince and myself on more than one occasion. Such as the countless times when Jared and Steve Bannon went into the Oval without an appointment. Reince would be furious. His job was to clear every appointment someone had with the president. "How did this happen?" he would ask me. "Why didn't I know about this?"

Other times, after I had done something Jared or Steve had asked me to do without running it by Reince, the conversation would become rather unpleasant.

"Why did you do that?" Reince would ask.

"Jared told me to do it," I'd say.

"Well, Jared is not the chief of staff. I am."

No, he wasn't, but he was President Trump's son-in-law and senior advisor, and in this administration, that outranked the chief of staff.

Once Eric Trump came to have lunch with his dad; it had been on the schedule for a few days. The president was having a meeting with a foreign leader in the Cabinet Room that was running much longer than we'd thought it would. I didn't dare to interrupt.

The meeting came to an end eventually, but he was an hour behind schedule and now wouldn't be able to visit with his son.

"Reince," I said afterward, "Eric is very frustrated he didn't get to spend time with his dad. I think we need to keep the family in mind when they are here."

That set him off. "Well," he said, "maybe the Outer Oval team needs to do a better job of controlling the flow of the schedule, then."

Actually, it was clear from the start that Reince was the weakest link in the trifecta with Jared and Steve and the person most likely to go first.

The president gave him his position as a reward for the incredible job he had done in helping him get elected, but Reince believed in structure, while Jared and Steve preferred, as it's often been said, for Trump to be Trump.

Was the president aware of the conflict among the three top aides? Sure he was, and he didn't mind. He approaches aspects of the presidency similar to the way he ran *The Apprentice*. Only the strong move on. People say he thrives off chaos. That's not it. He's certain he will achieve the best results when people fight for what they believe in.

I empathized with Reince. His main problem was that running a political organization is different from running the federal government, especially with Donald Trump at the helm. The first chief of staff in this administration was bound to struggle.

At the RNC, everybody had called Reince "Chairman." He was the center of attention, one of the most powerful Republicans in the country. He was used to being stopped in airports and had body guys who acted like his security.

Now, at the White House, everyone just called him "Reince." I have to believe he felt a lessening of authority. Being White House chief of staff is usually a step up. Not in this case. The president was his own chief of staff, and, knowing him as well as I do, I'm certain he still is. He constantly reviewed his schedule before any meetings were confirmed and always made the final call.

It was not long before the president lost confidence in Reince. I often heard him complain to his guests in the Oval Office how Reince had no control over the West Wing.

The president was never shy about telling us what he thought about anyone, including those who had literally just walked out the door. He seemed disappointed with just about everyone at one point or another.

Did it bother me? Not at all. In most cases, I agreed with him. The person he was angry with *had* been annoying or insubordinate.

Not that he couldn't be gracious, regardless of how he felt. Take, for instance, the Speaker of the House, Nancy Pelosi, not exactly his favorite person in the world.

One day, the president called me into the dining room to dictate me a letter that he wanted to send her.

"Dear Nancy," he started.

I thought *"Yes! This is going to be epic."*

The letter is one you may remember in which, during the government shutdown in January 2019, he informed her that she couldn't use a federally funded military aircraft for a trip overseas.

*"This is freaking amazing,"* I kept thinking as he dictated.

Yet whenever the Speaker came into the Oval Office, he treated her with tremendous respect. Five minutes before, he had been talking about how awful she was. You would never have known it.

Nancy, in fact, was one of the first calls he placed on election night in 2018. He called to congratulate the new speaker of the House. I overheard his side of their conversation, and it was genuine. The president said he thought they could get something great accomplished if they worked together.

As the months dragged on, his working relationship with Reince Priebus grew more tenuous. The president set up more of his own appointments and meetings. "I'm going to do this, Madeleine," he said on many occasions. "You don't need to tell Reince."

I didn't, needless to say. I had chosen sides long before, and I wasn't about to change my allegiance now. That would have been disastrous. The president, as I saw it, had every right to go around Reince. If the chief of staff, like any other staffer, doesn't continue to earn his respect, he has no other choice. Even so, up until the very end, Reince still acted as if he were in complete control.

In late July, six months into the administration, it was official: Reince was out.

It wasn't shocking. Then again, it was. Almost immediately I went to the chief of staff suite, which was filled with former RNC folks. Until someone suggested we get back to work; it wouldn't look good us all to be seen gathered there.

Reince was far from naive. He'd known that his days in the White House were coming to an end, but he was a human being, and how he learned his fate must have been hard on him. It came in a sequence of tweets during a presidential trip, and once Air Force One arrived at Andrews Air Force Base, Reince rode back to the White House separately from the motorcade. There, once again, was an example of how fleeting power really is: here one minute, gone the next.

Even so, Reince was not my focus. I worried instead about what would happen to me. I had distanced myself from Reince in recent months, but I was in the White House because of him. Would I be the next to go?

Mercifully, I didn't have to wait long. The next day, I saw General Kelly, Reince's replacement, in the residence when the president had some people over for a movie.

"You're staying, right?" he asked.

"If you'll have me, sir," I said.

General Kelly and his staff reassured me over the next week or so that I was a crucial member of the team. I don't think that would have been the case if I had aligned myself too closely with Reince.

Sadly, I don't have much of a relationship with my former boss these days. As with Katie, I was grateful to have his support.

Take, for example, when it came out that three other former RNC staffers in the West Wing and I were making $20,000 less than others in similar positions. Reince's assistant brought it to his attention, and he dealt with it immediately. That said all you needed to know about Reince. He takes care of his own.

After he left, he called me a few times but I didn't always call him back. Again I put power above friendship, and it was not until I was gone myself that I understood what it really feels like to be on the outside, praying you are still relevant.

To his credit, Reince remains an enthusiastic supporter of the president, helping to raise money for the RNC and the 2020 campaign.

I have never explained myself to Reince, as I did to Katie.

One day, I hope to be able to.

# CHAPTER THIRTEEN

# Some of the President's Men

A lot of men walked through the Outer Oval Office during my time there. Most of them I came to respect, even revere, so committed were they to the president and his policies. They weren't obligated to serve. They did it out of love for their country.

Needless to say, there were exceptions, those who were out only for their selfish interests. I could spot them a mile away.

One was Anthony Scaramucci, better known as "The Mooch." He was like a meteor, coming to the White House as director of communications on July 21, 2017, replacing Sean Spicer, and leaving on July 31. That surely has to go down as one of the shortest—and most contentious—stays of anyone ever in the West Wing.

Anthony had always been convinced it was Reince who had kept him from getting a job in the White House, and he made it very clear that the chief of staff wouldn't stand in his way of getting close to the president. I had a bad feeling about Anthony before he joined the administration.

I wasn't surprised when he self-destructed. What sealed his fate was when he made foul comments about Steve Bannon and accused Reince of being a leaker, referring to him as a "paranoid schizophrenic." Reince was practically out the door by then, but kicking him when he was down revealed just what kind of guy Anthony is.

The White House was rid of him, but I wasn't. Even after he was ousted, Anthony called the president on a regular basis. You would think he might have been a bit humbled by such a public humiliation and maybe kept his distance for a while. You don't know Anthony.

One evening when he called, it was well after 10:00 p.m., and the president didn't usually like to take calls that late in the evening. He made exceptions, of course, whenever it was something really essential. This didn't fall into that category.

Except to Anthony. When I told him the president wasn't available, he exploded. "Madeleine," he said, "if I find out you are lying and just not putting me through, I'll make sure the president knows about it."

He was threatening me. The audacity of that guy.

"Okay, Anthony," I told him, "I will be more than happy to call and potentially wake up the president of the United States for whatever you need to say to him that is so urgent. Would you like me to do that?"

Crickets. Just what I'd expected.

Honestly, it is remarkable that Anthony lasted as long as he did, and it might have been even longer if General Kelly hadn't made his firing a condition for agreeing to replace Reince.

Believe it or not, Anthony was almost pleasant compared to one of the president's former lawyers, Michael Cohen, who went to prison for tax evasion and campaign finance violations. Michael was friendly to anyone he thought could benefit him. To everyone else, he was a tyrant. He terrified me from day one.

I will never forget the time he called about his daughter, who was starting an internship in the first lady's office. She had shown up at the White House gate but hadn't filed the necessary paperwork properly. Michael called me right away. "The Secret Service won't let her in," he said. "You need to do something about it."

"There's no way I can leave my desk," I told him. Even if I went down there, I said, I still wouldn't be able to get her in. Everyone who enters the complex has to be vetted by the Secret Service. If your Social Security number or birthday is entered wrong, you can't get in. There are no exceptions.

As you might expect, Michael didn't take no for an answer. "If this doesn't get figured out," he went on, getting angrier by the minute, "I will call the president and first lady and say you weren't helpful."

He could call whomever he wanted. The president was working in the Oval Office, which meant I wasn't leaving my desk.

So, get this, he reached out next to Lindsay Reynolds, and when she told him she couldn't help, either, he threatened her, as well. "If you don't take care of my daughter," he warned, "you'll be scraping gum off the sidewalk by the time I'm done with you."

It came as no surprise when both Anthony Scaramucci and Michael Cohen turned on the president the first chance they could. Why does it always seem that the most outspoken Trump "loyalists" are the first to turn on him when things don't go their way?

That's who they are, I suppose—and you wonder why the president trusts so few people? He pretended it didn't bother him, but I know it did. How could it not? Especially when it came to Michael, who had worked at the Trump Organization for a decade.

Again, one should keep in mind that unlike anybody else who has attained the highest office in the land, President Trump has been a celebrity for more than forty years. Fame invites enemies, tons of them, and he was no exception. Though it wasn't until he declared himself a Republican and ran for president that the same elites who had long enjoyed his company now saw him as an easy target.

And I thought politicians were hypocrites.

Not that he made it easy on himself. At times he got stuck on matters others thought he should have left alone.

Such as the issue over how many people had attended his inauguration. He talked about it for months afterward. No one was still bothered by it, except him.

I understood, though, why he was so frustrated. Instead of giving him his moment in history, as they have with every other president, the media turned their attention to the women's marches that had taken place in DC and around the world the day after. The press would never give him a break.

I ended up putting up three enlarged photos from the inauguration for him to see whenever he walked through the hallway leading out of the Outer Oval Office. I knew how happy they would make him. The photos were beautiful and showed the tens of thousands of people who had come to support him. Unlike the other "jumbos" in the West Wing, which were switched out on a regular basis, I never changed those three photos.

The president knows that there is a group of people who will never be supportive for no other reason than they just don't like his personality, but instead of continually trying to win them over, he doubles down on his rhetoric and policy. That is another reason I admire him so much. He doesn't play the games the politicians play. He's not one of *them*.

Which brings me back to Senator Lindsey Graham.

The night Lindsey called to say he was on his way to the White House with Senator Cruz and Senator Sasse was far from a one-time occurrence. He constantly took advantage of the president.

Whenever they spoke, their conversation would undoubtedly come around to golf. Lindsey is an excellent golfer, and the president does enjoy playing with him. The next thing I knew, I would receive a call from Lindsey's assistant. "The president just invited the senator to play golf on Saturday," his assistant would say. "Can you provide any details?"

I'd heard every word of their conversation. The president hadn't exactly invited Lindsey to play; Lindsey had all but invited himself, and the president, being the gracious man he is, had agreed.

On occasion, out of nowhere, Lindsey would go on the attack. How, I wondered, could he play golf with the president one day and criticize him in public the next? He was a politician, that's how, though he would have shown a lot more character if, like Senator Sasse, he had given the president a heads-up before he blasted a certain policy.

Still, when other staff members or I flagged the latest Lindsey attack for the president, he didn't pay much attention.

For every occasion Lindsey was critical, there were five other times he was behind the president 1,000 percent. Overall, he is a fierce advocate for the administration, and it was better to have him on the team, where he could be controlled to some degree, than on the outside. That was true of a lot of people on the Hill.

What the president could not tolerate was when anyone on his team tried to go around him.

There is no better example than his former national security advisor John Bolton. Whenever the president wanted something done that wasn't on Bolton's agenda, Bolton would try to squash it. Someone forgot to tell Bolton that Donald Trump is the president, not him.

I can't tell you how many times a call request from a head of state came through my desk and the initial response from Bolton's team on the NSC (National Security Council) was that the president should not take the call at all or wait for a couple of days before returning it. Bolton was stalling; it was as simple as that.

It placed me in a terribly awkward position, to the point I decided that enough was enough. I ignored the NSC's "recommendations," telling the president about the call request as soon as I could. He, not John Bolton, should decide if and when he would talk to a foreign leader. Once the call got scheduled, everybody who needed to would have the opportunity to brief the president.

Bolton was always causing trouble. Such as the time the president asked him to send a note to Chinese president Xi Jinping, whom he often referred to as "king" since he is the president for life. The president loved to send handwritten notes, often on a clipping from a newspaper or magazine article. If it was a positive piece, the note was complimentary.

Once, a *New York Times* article had the headline "Despite Endorsement, Trump Keeps Asking: Is Vice President Loyal?" The president wrote: "Mike—Total Bull—Fake News," with his signature underneath. Other times, if a story upset him, he might write, "Not good. Fix this!"

Another time, Canadian prime minister Justin Trudeau was on the cover of *Bloomberg Businessweek* magazine with the headline "The Anti-Trump." "Looking good, hope it's not true," the president wrote on the magazine cover, which he then sent to Trudeau.

Anyway, two weeks after he had written the note to President Xi, when he asked if it had been delivered, Bolton said no. President Trump wasn't thrilled, to put it mildly, especially since Bolton didn't have a good reason for not having delivered it. Perhaps he was hoping the president would be too busy to bring it up again.

It wasn't the first time that kind of thing happened. For example, I would give a note to the staff secretary, who would say he couldn't send it because a policy the article referred to in the note was incorrect or he didn't think it was an appropriate way to communicate with a foreign leader.

Guess who had to hear about it.

"I asked you to send the letter," the president would tell me.

"They said they couldn't do it," I would reply.

"Don't give it to anyone else," he'd say. "Just send it."

Which was what I did.

I wish this type of resistance—I might even call it a rebellion—was rare in the West Wing. Sadly, it was not. Those people felt they were preventing a disaster by not sending out a note the president asked to be sent or not following through on other direct orders. They told themselves they were saving him from himself.

Please. Donald Trump didn't need to be saved. He needed people to do what he asked. I felt like saying to them: If this note is so bad, send it out anyway, and let him face the criticism. He can handle it. That went for letters, tweets, statements, and other communications.

I understood if they wanted to discuss their concerns. Perhaps there was an update in legislation or in negotiations that the president wasn't yet aware of, and sending a note to or speaking with a foreign leader too soon would cause a problem.

Yet there's a big difference between saying "Madeleine, please let me know if the president is going to call Prime Minister Abe [of Japan], as I'd like to brief him ahead of time" and "Don't let the president call Prime Minister Abe."

I'm not suggesting that his advisors shouldn't weigh in. Of course they should. Otherwise, what is the purpose of having them there? The president needs to hear every side of an issue before making a decision, and, as I said before, if you make a compelling case, he might change his mind. But once he makes his decision, the discussion is over. If you don't approve, get a job in a think tank or look for one in the private sector. He will easily find someone to replace you.

People thought that if they ignored an order, the president would forget about it. If there was one thing that stood out to me about my time in the White House, it was that Donald Trump doesn't forget anything.

Once, he asked, "When am I having lunch with Franklin Graham and his family?" Franklin Graham is the son of Billy Graham, the late evangelist.

With the typical chaos in the West Wing, I had forgotten to schedule the lunch. I answered, "Soon!" and immediately picked up the phone to set it up.

Bolton also kept the strangest hours. He got to his office in the West Wing hours before most people and often took off around four or five o'clock. That wasn't in sync with a president who arrived much later and left much later. Many times, when the president asked me to have Bolton come to the Oval Office, I had to tell him he'd already gone home.

★

I knew my place, which meant I stayed away from sensitive matters, such as national security and intelligence briefings. The door to the Oval Office was closed for those types of meetings. No staffers handed me notes to take in. I dared not interrupt unless it was absolutely necessary.

Yet there was one sensitive matter I couldn't stay away from. No one could. It was there, always.

Russia.

I don't pretend to possess any special insight, but I can tell you the huge toll it took on the president, day after day. He was innocent, but he still had to defend himself against those outrageous charges.

If he received bad news about the investigation in the morning, which happened too often, it affected his mood for the rest of the day. People have no idea how much of his time it occupied, time that should have been spent on serving the American people. The same goes for the Democrats on the Hill. Rather than focusing on the issues that matter, they set up committee after committee for nothing more than political gain.

Rarely did a day pass when I didn't hear from a member of his legal team, asking for one more call, one more meeting, many toward the end of the day: "We need two more hours with him every day for the rest of the week."

Two more hours? Are you serious? The president has been working since six o'clock every morning. Could you please give him a break?

It felt as though they lived there, the way his attorney Jay Sekulow and the others took over the private dining room, drafting statements, making edits, popping into the Oval Office every minute or two to show him something.

No wonder it got to the president. It would get to anyone.

"Goddamn Russia hoax," I heard him say more times than I can count.

If something on the news ticked him off, which happened quite a bit because the coverage was so unfairly negative, he would blurt out, "Call Jay and tell him that's not true."

Finally, when the hard work of Jay's incredible team paid off and the Mueller Report proved no collusion, the sense of relief was palpable. We could focus now on the work the people had elected the president to do. The Democrats had wasted all that time and money for nothing.

The lawyers came into the Oval Office, everyone hugging everyone else. There had been times when we had wondered if that moment would ever come.

"Jay," I joked, "I'm so excited I won't see you again for a while."

Fast-forward to last fall, when it came out during the Ukraine fiasco that I had connected Rudy Giuliani to Secretary Pompeo since he wasn't able to get through via the "proper channels."

The press made it appear as if there had been something sinister in my putting them together.

To the contrary. Rudy was one of the president's attorneys, and I had vowed never to ask questions when a matter involved the president and his legal team. I just provided them with whatever they needed. I would have connected Rudy, Jay, or anyone else on the team with just about anyone they asked me to.

To be honest, seeing the Ukraine story unfold, I was, for the first time, glad I had left the West Wing shortly before it broke in September. Given what so many of my colleagues went through during the Russia investigation—the subpoenas, testimonies, and money spent on legal fees—I would have worried about the possibility of being subpoenaed myself.

At the same time, I felt awful for the president. Now he had to cope with another "scandal."

Would it have made a difference if I had still been there?

Not on the policy side, obviously.

Yet I have no doubt that I could have been a voice of comfort during a very trying time. I could have told him what few people did: "Sir, you are doing a great job. We will get through this. Stay strong, and keep fighting."

★

One night in November 2018, long before the Russia matter had been settled, I was sitting at my desk when I noticed the line dedicated to the Oval suite on my phone light up. The president was calling from the dining room.

"Madeleine, come in here and bring your pad," he said.

Boy, did I love hearing that, no matter what time it was. Don't get me wrong, I loved arranging his calls, setting up his meetings, and keeping the trains on the track. Nothing I did, however, was as rewarding as taking dictation. It gave me a chance to spend quality time with him. Moreover, whatever he said was bound to turn into a controversial tweet or letter that would make the Democrats go ballistic. How good is that? Yet I must admit I was nervous every time. I didn't want to mess up.

That evening, for some reason, everybody else had left the Outer Oval, and the rest of the West Wing was unusually quiet. It was just the president and myself in the dining room. He read me the first draft of a statement he was working on related to Jamal Khashoggi, the Saudi Arabian freelance journalist and critic of Saudi Arabia, who had been murdered in the Saudi Consulate in Istanbul, Turkey.

The president was torn. For anyone to suggest that he didn't care about Khashoggi's death is absurd. He cared a great deal. Still, he had to balance that with not wanting to risk antagonizing Saudi Arabia, a valuable ally.

As he read what he had written, I quickly scribbled every word in my notebook. When he was done, I went to my computer to type it up, praying I would be able to read my own handwriting.

"Go fast," he said.

I brought it back to him as quickly as I could. He made some edits, and I typed it again.

We went back and forth for an hour, perhaps longer, the president's valet coming in every so often to refresh his Diet Coke. Yes, Donald Trump talks off the cuff a lot of the time, but don't be fooled; no one else I've ever been around pays more attention to the details.

That includes the placement of every comma and exclamation point and which words he chooses to capitalize. He often said that he was creating a new language. By the time, I left the job, I was instinctively capitalizing words such as Country, Military, and Witch Hunt.

Finally, he was satisfied.

The statement, in part, referred to the murder as an "unacceptable and horrible crime" but said that the United States would "remain a steadfast partner of Saudi Arabia to ensure the interests of our country, Israel and all other partners in the region. It is our paramount goal to fully eliminate the threat of terrorism throughout the world!"

"Put it out," the president said.

That was where I was out of my element. I didn't put things out. Put it out where? How?

I called Sarah Sanders. "We've got to get this out," I told her.

It was way too long, she said, even for a statement. It was four pages. Most statements are one, or two at the most.

Soon—surprise, surprise—John Bolton got involved. "We can't put this out," he said.

Bolton didn't intimidate me. Not with the president in my corner. "Well, he wants it out," I said.

Before long, one person after another came into the Oval Office, arguing that the statement was too much in favor of Saudi Arabia or did not condemn the murder enough. This will cause quite a stir, they said.

Too bad. The statement went out exactly as the president wanted it.

Afterward, though, I caught some flak from Derek Lyons, the staff secretary. "Why didn't you call and bring me into this?" he asked.

I'd been so busy working with the president, I told him, that I hadn't had a moment to stop and think of asking anyone else for input.

I also believe the president had me work on it alone for a reason. He didn't want feedback—resistance—from others. They would have wanted to push him to be stronger, in one direction or the other, and what he needed was to strike the right balance between empathy for the victim and standing with our ally. I might have suggested a word or two, but I wouldn't have objected to the premise.

The president could've asked for anyone else in the West Wing: Sarah, Dan, Kellyanne, Jared, Derek, Bolton. The list is endless.

He didn't. He asked for me.

Who was I, anyway? An expert in the Middle East? Hardly. Someone trained in the art of diplomacy? Not quite. To this president, however, in that moment in time, that was not what mattered.

I think of that night a lot these days, about the trust he placed in me, a young woman at the outset of her career. He believed in me, perhaps more than I believed in myself, and for that I will always be grateful.

## CHAPTER FOURTEEN

# *We Are Women, Hear Us Roar*

More than anything else, even the tweets, whenever I told people, young women especially, about my job at the White House, they would ask me, "How can you work for that man?"

Even the way they put it—*that man*—made it sound as if he were the Devil.

Or they would refer to him derisively as "Trump," rarely "President Trump." The lack of respect for both the man and the office was beyond belief. They reminded me of the media, still unable to get over the fact that their beloved Hillary Clinton had lost.

At the same time, I understood where they were coming from. I had been there myself, forming my initial opinion based solely on what I heard or read in the news.

As you know, I had come around pretty quickly to seeing a different side of the man, a side of him that the media will never bother to acknowledge. It was, by the way, a side even others in the West Wing didn't often see. I saw the tremendous respect he has for women and how much he relies on them. The evidence is overwhelming.

For one thing, he has put one woman after another into a position of responsibility in every part of the administration. As a matter of fact, at the beginning of 2019, his third year in office, the president had more high-level female advisors than Obama, George W. Bush, or Clinton had at the same stage.

The most shining example is Gina Haspel. She should be a household name, an icon girls everywhere look up to. She isn't, and I blame the press. Believe me, if another president instead of President Trump had made Gina the first female director of the CIA, there would have been no end to the positive coverage. You will never hear a word about that from Gina, though. She is a quiet professional who works incredibly hard.

Another woman he placed a lot of trust in is Nikki Haley, the former governor of South Carolina, whom he nominated to be our ambassador to the United Nations. I felt a real connection to her, having gone to college in the Palmetto State.

So many people, in fact, were impressed by Nikki that there was speculation the president would put her, not Vice President Pence, onto the ticket in 2020. I have no idea if he was seriously considering it, although he once asked me, "Madeleine, what do you think about this business of replacing Mike with Nikki?"

"You and the vice president have something very special," I said. "You should stick with him."

"You're probably right."

Whatever my response, I would never assume it swayed him one way or the other. Although the president constantly asked others for their opinions, he relied on his own judgment, and he was usually right.

The clearest evidence, though, of his true feelings toward women is how he treated me, someone who came into his administration without the credentials of a Gina Haspel or a Nikki Haley.

It started with the dinner that first weekend at Bedminster, when I was there to take care of Reince and Katie. He had no idea who I was, yet he was extremely kind and gracious.

Then, a month later, he took the time to call me up to his office to say I was doing a great job as the greeter girl in Trump Tower.

Once I got to the Outer Oval Office, he made me feel valuable, and that was true the entire time I was there. Every once in a while, he even asked what was going on in my personal life, how Ben and I were doing, for example. He wasn't just trying to be polite. He genuinely cared.

One day in December 2018 stands out. Jordan Karem, one of the president's aides, had announced he was leaving the West Wing, opening the door for me to seek the promotion I'd been eyeing for months. I only prayed that things would go better than they had in the spring, the last time that job was available. That was when Jordan became director of Oval Office operations. I had been upset and confused and had gone to see Joe Hagin, who was the deputy chief of staff for operations and in charge of White House personnel.

If I had known that Joe was looking for someone, no doubt I would have wanted to be considered. With John McEntee, Hope Hicks, and Keith Schiller, the first director of Oval Office operations, gone, I was the only person in the Outer Oval Office who had been there from the start. That had to count for something.

I told Joe as much, and his response was appalling. He practically laughed in my face. "You're not qualified for that job," he told me. "You're way too young."

Not qualified? I had been doing the job in everything but title for months, and as far as I could tell, there had been no complaints. As for being "too young," have you looked around the building lately, Joe? This is an administration with a twenty-nine-year-old communications director—a female, I might add—and others from my generation in senior positions.

Besides, I didn't believe him for a minute. It had nothing to do with my age and everything to do with my gender.

Joe had held the same position under President George W. Bush, and knew a great deal about how a White House should operate, which was invaluable. Except he wasn't willing to adapt to how this president liked to operate. He saw me as a secretary, nothing more.

Still, there was nothing I could do except keep my mouth shut and serve the president as well as possible.

Some mornings, though, before he came down from the residence, I walked to the East Wing, where the first lady and her staff worked. I often had a legitimate reason for going over there, such as dropping off paperwork or picking up gifts, but I really went there to visit with Lindsay Reynolds and the other women in the office.

When I was with them, I felt supported, empowered, which wasn't always the case in the West Wing.

★

Fast-forward to December, when Jordan decided to leave. Nick Luna, who had been on the president's advance team, was chosen to join us in the Outer Oval Office and had been told he would be given the title I coveted.

I didn't blame Nick—he was ambitious, like everyone else in the West Wing—but I was starting to question if I would ever get the chance to be more than just an assistant. I knew that in the president's eyes, I was much more than that. Why couldn't the rest of the West Wing see it?

Feeling out of options, I approached three women in the building for advice: Ivanka, Kellyanne, and Sarah. If anybody would know how to best navigate this delicate situation, it would be them.

I admired each woman, for different reasons.

I admired Ivanka for the character and class she has continuously shown since moving to Washington, where she has been unfairly criticized merely because of the fact that her father is the president. She is always poised and treats everyone she meets with great respect.

I looked up to her, as well, for being able to find common ground with people in the White House with sharply different views. Ivanka would fit in well with any administration, Republican or Democrat.

Most impressive to me, though, is the job Ivanka and Jared have done as parents. They are very dedicated to their work, but the kids always come first. The president is blessed to have them, as are their three beautiful children.

As for Kellyanne, no one has been a more outspoken advocate for Donald Trump, and no one has taken more abuse for it. Don't tell me the fact she is a woman has nothing to do with it. The media would never go after a man as savagely. They should be ashamed of themselves. Amazingly, it hasn't deterred her one bit. People forget that Kellyanne is the first woman to have run a successful presidential campaign.

She has also had to cope with her husband, George, an attorney, who attacks the president every opportunity he gets. The press is one thing, but how Kellyanne can handle criticism from somebody in her own household without letting it affect her work is beyond me.

Then there is Sarah. The way she was treated, it is hard to believe, was even more shameful. To return to the podium day after day after people poked fun at her was incredibly brave. I would never have been able to demonstrate as much composure and grace.

She is a rock star. When the president and his staff went to Ireland in June 2019, several of us went to a local pub one evening. Everyone recognized Sarah and wanted pictures with her. When I brought my family or friends to the White House, they were almost as excited about meeting her as about meeting the president.

I'm not sure anyone in the West Wing made more sacrifices. During spring break with her husband and three children in 2019, probably the first time she had taken time off in years, she was on the phone all day, every day. Striking the right balance was impossible. Sometimes, in the early afternoon, she would leave for the day to keep an obligation with her kids. She risked not being around when the president needed her, but she wouldn't risk not being around for her kids.

Although I was devastated to see her go, I was happy for her when she made the decision that was obviously right for her. As rewarding as it is to work in the White House, the pressures and scrutiny are unmatched. You can take it for only so long before it begins to overwhelm you. I admire Sarah more than I can possibly express.

You can see why I sought the counsel of those three remarkable women. Each has had to prove herself over and over. Having female role models like them, in addition to Katie, Hope, Lindsay, and many others, filled me with confidence.

The question I posed to each of them was the same: Should I approach the president about the new title?

Their answer, without the slightest hesitation: Yes!

The president doesn't care if you are a man or woman, they told me. What matters is whether or not you do a good job, and if you do, he will take care of you. That has long been his approach in business and entertainment and now in government.

Kellyanne put it best: "No one in the White House is going to fight for you. If you want something, you are going to have to fight for it yourself. Go see him!"

That was exactly the pep talk I needed.

One morning, a couple of weeks before Jordan's final day and Nick's first, I waited for the president in the Outer Oval Office. As usual, he arrived around eleven with Jordan, who was also his body man. I waited for Jordan to leave. I needed to be alone with the president.

He headed straight to the dining room to read the papers and watch the news. I hated to bother him during that time, but I was not certain when I might get another chance. "Sir, can I speak with you privately for a minute?" I asked.

"Of course, come in," he said.

I was nervous, to say the least, and in a way different from ever before. I was always asking him about someone else. Now I would be asking about me.

No matter what Ivanka, Kellyanne, and Sarah said, I was still taking a big risk. How many people ever ask the president of the United States for a promotion? What if he were to say no? What if he told me I was out of line for coming straight to him? Would that hurt our relationship, perhaps for good?

There was no need to tell him the entire story. The president didn't have all the time in the world. I knew that better than anyone.

I told him how much it would mean to me to get a promotion. I didn't want to leave the White House, whenever that was, without having served as anything more than an executive assistant. If he, as expected, gained a second term and I stayed until the end, I would be in my midthirties by then.

Don't worry, I told him, I will keep doing my current job, only with a few additional responsibilities. You won't even know the difference. It's just a change in my title. I am not even asking for a raise.

He listened patiently until I was done. "That sounds good," he said, and that was all it took. The title would soon be mine: Director of Oval Office Operations.

I walked out of the dining room feeling much as I had when I had walked out of his office in Trump Tower two Decembers earlier, when he had given me that first compliment. On top of the world.

The only downside was what occurred afterward, as a rumor spread that I had lobbied the president's kids—Ivanka, Eric, and Don, Jr.—for the title and that I had gone to the residence uninvited to speak to the president.

It was the most ridiculous lie of my entire time in the West Wing, and that's saying a lot.

★

You can complain about some of the comments he's made about women over the years, but when it came down to it, he stood up for me, just as he has stood up for Kellyanne, Sarah, Hope, and countless other women he has surrounded himself with, both in the White House and in his previous life.

Yes, he has said things he should not have said, but he comes from a different generation, when men said things like that all the time. He shouldn't be penalized because the times have changed. His heart is always in the right place, and that is what matters most.

Besides, look how much he does to help women. There is one example after another. He commuted the prison sentence of Alice Johnson, who was serving a mandatory life sentence for a nonviolent drug offense. The work he has done to combat the opioid epidemic, with the passage of the Caring Recovery for Infants and Babies (CRIB) Act, has funded Brigid's Path, a facility that aids women and their babies who struggle with substance abuse. The president has also signed legislation to combat human trafficking, which affects tens of thousands of women every year. I could go on and on.

On the other hand, former president Bill Clinton was considered a big supporter of women's issues. I think you get the point.

Where does President Trump's respect for women come from? That's not for me to say, but I do believe it stems from the deep reverence he held for his mother. What I can tell you is that I saw his respect for women day after day.

Nonetheless, that hasn't stopped his haters from suggesting that a lust for women is the reason he keeps them around.

"The president just likes brunettes," people have said.

Some, including members of my own family, even asked if the president or anyone else in Washington had ever said or done anything inappropriate. Absolutely not. Never. I can't think of a single occasion when I felt the least bit uncomfortable in his presence.

From time to time, he would compliment me on my outfit or tell me I looked nice. I would hear him on the phone with friends say, "Isn't Madeleine great? She is so lovely."

Yet I always felt those comments were endearing, not offensive. I would contend that anyone, man or woman, enjoys hearing a compliment every once in a while. Though there is a lot about the Me Too movement that I applaud, it's gone a bit too far.

★

The most vivid proof of Donald Trump's admiration for women can be summed up in two words: Melania Trump.

I will always remember the night I met her. It was at Mar-a-Lago during the transition. The president-elect, as he had at Bedminster, invited several of us to join him for dinner. When I sat down, directly across the table, there she was, more stunning than ever.

She reminded me of a porcelain doll, so wonderfully put together. I was afraid that if I touched her, she might break. I didn't know it at the time, but nothing could ever break that woman. She is that strong.

No, she doesn't generate the attention that Michelle Obama or even Laura Bush did, but that is by design. Getting attention doesn't interest her. She cherishes her privacy.

In October 2018, I was a member of the advance team for Mrs. Trump's weeklong journey to Africa. It was her first solo international trip as the first lady. She visited Ghana, Malawi, Egypt, and Kenya.

I was dying to go and was grateful when Lindsay Reynolds signed off on it. I went to Kenya, where I helped prepare for her trip to an elephant orphanage and to see a performance at the Kenya National Theatre. She also went on a safari and enjoyed tea with Margaret Kenyatta, Kenya's first lady.

Mrs. Trump showed tremendous dignity at every official function she attended. Yet it was during the unscripted moments that she was at her best, especially if children were around. Her face lit up. English not being her first language, she can be very reserved, but with children, language isn't necessary. She communicates with a touch, a smile, her feelings for them impossible to miss. You can't orchestrate that kind of connection. Either it is real or it isn't.

I was also moved by her love for her own son. Barron comes before anything else.

The first lady, you might recall, got a lot of criticism for not moving into the White House right after the inauguration. Some people even suggested that she was going to stay in New York indefinitely. That was never going to happen. She was simply being a responsible parent, refusing to disrupt her ten-year-old boy's life in the middle of the school year. Believe it or not, some things are more important than living in the White House—even if your husband is the president.

No wonder everyone loves working for her. The first lady is how most women would like to see themselves: compassionate, independent, and generous.

She showed how independent she is simply by making the trip, as it came not long after the president had made some rather harsh comments about countries in Africa. Bottom line: Mrs. Trump is very much her own person.

The president, who is so proud of her, sees the same virtues, and I am convinced that's a big reason why they're perfect for each other. She never hesitates to challenge him, to call him out if necessary.

So if women want to know how I could have worked for Donald Trump, it's easy. He puts women into leadership positions. He promotes them whenever he can. He seeks out their advice. And he is married to a woman who sets her own course.

*That man* is the best supporter a woman could ever have.

# CHAPTER FIFTEEN

# A Test of Faith

The first time I heard General John Kelly speak in public was in early June of 2017. The scene couldn't have been more emotional.

President Trump and the first lady were welcoming Gold Star Families to the White House for a ceremony in the East Room to honor heroic men and women who died in service to their nation. The term "Gold Star" goes back as far as World War I, but this was the first time a ceremony like this had ever taken place at the White House.

The room, lit by candlelight, was gorgeous, and the music, performed by the United States Marine Band was incredibly moving. A military soloist sang a beautiful rendition of "The Battle Hymn of the Republic" and "America the Beautiful."

The president addressed the families before he yielded the floor to General Kelly, then secretary of homeland security. The general spoke about his son, First Lieutenant Robert Kelly, who had been killed in 2010 when he stepped on a land mine in

Afghanistan. He asked the family members in the audience to stand as their loved one was named in honor.

Later, while he was chief of staff, General Kelly left the White House on occasion to go by himself to Arlington National Cemetery to visit his son's grave and walk on those hallowed grounds. The general was under a tremendous amount of pressure. My guess is that the visits helped give him the perspective to keep going. He seemed at peace when he returned.

I could hardly breathe that evening in the East Room. Listening to the general and gazing at the faces of those who were grieving, it occurred to me that war doesn't discriminate among the young men and women it takes from us.

When General Kelly replaced Reince nearly two months later, I welcomed the change. We needed some discipline in the White House, no one could dispute that, and who better to instill that than a retired marine four-star general? He enlisted in the marine corps in 1970, serving in a variety of key posts, including as the leader of the US Southern Command, which ran our military operations in South America, Central America, and the Caribbean.

I believe the president's tremendous respect for the military is what drew him to General Kelly in the first place. During the campaign, he promised to increase the size of the army, navy, marine corps, and air force. He kept his promise, that's for sure. We are more prepared than ever for any crisis overseas.

But what was important wasn't just making sure that our nation's military branches had enough funds; the president wanted the men and women in the armed services to know how much he appreciated the sacrifices they were making. He took the time to get to know his military aides and Air Force One crew, and anyone else who was affiliated with the military. When they came in for a departure photo with him, he asked them about their lives and careers and where they would be stationed next.

"Take care of yourself, and let us know if you need anything," he would tell them. "We're so proud of you."

General Kelly's impact on the West Wing was immediate. I recently looked at one of my journals, and what I wrote on September 4 summed it up:

> Kelly wasted no time laying down the law . . . and it was amazing! Everyone on staff listens to him and respects him, even the repeat offenders that Reince could never control.

By "repeat offenders," I was referring to those in the building who figured they could march into the Oval Office at any moment without an official appointment. Those unplanned visits put the president behind schedule and made it impossible for him to catch up. That chaos quickly came to an end when General Kelly took over—for a while, at least.

When Reince was chief of staff, roughly a dozen people showed up for the daily intelligence briefing. That was way too many. Under the new regime, that number went down to about five. I finally had someone to help me keep the trains on the track.

He also did a wonderful job of staffing the president, making sure every angle of an issue was represented in meetings. If the trade group was coming in, the general would have the "globalists," such as the former director of the National Economic Council, Gary Cohn, along with the "nationalists," such as Peter Navarro, the president's main trade advisor, in the room with the cabinet secretaries. You can't ask for much more from a chief of staff.

I was thrilled on a personal level, as well. I liked him the moment we met when I was the greeter girl. I had been used to booking travel arrangements for the principals, often dealing only with their assistants. That wasn't the case with General Kelly. It was just him and me.

"I'll drive myself," he said. "Just tell me when and where."

The only other thing he needed to know was where he could change into a suit once he arrived in Bedminster.

His second interview was at Trump Tower. He took the train up from DC, and, again I asked if I could book his transportation.

No, thanks, he said. He walked from Penn Station to Trump Tower—in the rain, no less. Talk about low maintenance.

Months later, at the White House Christmas party, I introduced him to Ben. We'd been dating for just a few months. The general did everything but threaten Ben, a fellow marine officer, to take good care of me. Nothing like having a four-star general and White House chief of staff warn the boyfriend.

★

When did it go wrong? When did General Kelly fall out of favor, as Reince had? I can't pinpoint the precise day, although I clearly remember when I began to have my own doubts about him. Those doubts would become severe enough that I would question whether the White House was the right place for me, after all.

It was February 2018. I was used to the unexpected. You have to be if you work there.

The news that day was more unexpected than ever. Rob Porter, President Trump's first staff secretary, was being accused of physical and verbal abuse by not just one of his former wives, but two.

You could have handed me a list of everybody in the West Wing, and Rob would have been the last person I would have suspected of something like that. Rob was even-tempered and considerate, and I never saw him show anything less than total respect for women in the building. What's more, he was in a relationship with Hope Hicks. Hope would not have dated someone who was an abuser.

I got along with Rob pretty well, though we had our share of battles. The staff secretary was always bringing in documents for the president to read or sign. As the gatekeeper, I was bound to collide with him.

"This isn't a good time," I would often tell him.

"I just need five minutes," he would say.

"Okay, fine, go in, but hurry."

Rob and I worked together on keeping Peter Navarro from causing too much trouble. It was a challenge. Peter didn't properly vet documents and often went rogue on TV. Worse yet, he disrespected members of the staff, often raising his voice. He wasn't one of my favorite people.

Rob told me to call him each time Peter came to see the president in the Oval Office. He worried that Peter would pass along inaccurate information, and with good reason. I'm sure Peter eventually caught on to what I was doing. It was no coincidence that Rob kept showing up five minutes after he did.

At any rate, it wasn't the allegations against Rob that angered me the most. It was the way the White House—General Kelly, specifically—handled the matter.

Instead of adopting a neutral, wait-and-see attitude, the general's first response was to support Rob, who left the building but was allowed to work from home. I'm not suggesting that I thought Rob was guilty, just that it shouldn't have been assumed he was innocent, either.

I wasn't the only person in the building who was taken aback. With the way the West Wing was laid out, everybody practically sat on top of everybody else. You think you know the people you work with, but really you don't. Add the fact that we spent more time there than we did at home, and no wonder news about one of us would cause such a shock to our system.

The most affected, not surprisingly, was Hope, and I believe it was one of the reasons that she left the White House, along with the stress of having to testify in front of Congress on the Russia investigation. Reporters were staked outside her apartment. It all became unbearable.

I thought I would get over my misgivings after a couple of days, but when I didn't, I decided I'd better talk to someone. If anything, I was feeling worse. Rob had resigned by that point, but it didn't make a difference. How, I kept asking myself, can I work for somebody who initially downplayed those allegations? The way the president had handled the situation also gave me cause for concern. He had said things such as "This isn't the Rob I know." Apparently, it wasn't the Rob *any* of us knew.

Needless to say, I couldn't talk to anyone in the office. I wasn't sure how they felt about the issue and whether they would share my feelings with anyone else.

Instead, I asked the White House physician to set me up with an in-house psychologist. I am a firm believer in therapy, having started when I was a teenager. There should never be any shame in seeking help.

The psychologist I went to see was a woman; her office was in the Eisenhower Executive Office Building, next to the White House. She was a career person, not a Trump appointee. Even so, I was extremely careful in what I said about the president and General Kelly. You never know.

We met two or three times, and, to be honest, I didn't go there to tell her my life story. I had told my story to my therapist in California over and over, for years. I had gotten sick of hearing it myself. Telling it can be emotionally exhausting.

All I wanted was a chance to express my feelings without judgment. I needed to explore, with someone's help, what I truly thought of the president and his chief of staff and whether I could live with this concern. The answer I came to, was yes.

Don't get me wrong. I still believed they shouldn't have defended Rob in the manner they did, but the more I thought about it, the more it dawned on me how forgiving a man Donald Trump is. He wasn't excusing the abuse, if any did indeed occur. He was merely showing compassion for someone he was fond of.

Guess what. You can do both. Similarly to Jared, he believes in second chances. In the ensuing months, I occasionally heard the president ask how Rob was faring. Later, after I resigned, my friends in the White House said the president asked about me in the same warm manner. It meant a great deal to know he cared.

From time to time, I would think to myself, *I can't believe the president just said that*, but I never, for a second, doubted that he has a good heart. I always kept in mind the bigger picture, the good he does, day after day, for the American people.

What Sean Cairncross had told me at the RNC two days after the election, when I was about to quit and move back to California, applied now as much as ever. "Remember," he said, "it's much bigger than one person."

There was another reason, I must confess, why I came to terms with the Rob Porter matter, and it came down to one word: ambition.

To put it simply: I wanted to keep working at the White House, and if that meant making a deal with myself as to what I could or could not forgive, so be it.

Even so, from that moment on, my feelings about General Kelly were never quite the same.

A month later, John McEntee was forced to leave, another decision the general made that I found questionable. Why had Rob been permitted to resign a full day after the story about him broke, while John was asked to leave the property immediately.

★

There had been books before—quite a few, in fact, since the president had taken office, but no book like this.

The author was Bob Woodward, of Watergate fame, who has written about every president since Lincoln, or so it seems. In September 2018, word spread throughout the building that his book about the Trump White House would soon be hitting the shelves.

Unlike Michael Wolff's book, *Fire and Fury: Inside the Trump White House*, which had come out earlier that year and hadn't been well sourced, this one, from such an esteemed writer, would be taken seriously.

On the other hand, the Woodward book wasn't our top priority. Not even close. People assumed that whenever a book came out or a major article appeared in the *New York Times* or the *Washington Post*, we had a panic attack.

Hardly. We were too focused on other issues to pay attention to what an author wrote, even an author as respected as Woodward. When we got a copy of a book about the White House, I would go to the index to see if my name was there. That was what I worried about more than anything else, and that was likely true of other staffers. We could never be sure what would be written about us.

The president cared about the entire book, but not for the reason you might expect.

In the case of Woodward, he was upset that he had never spoken to him. The book, *Fear: Trump in the White House*, which became a number one best seller, was very critical of the administration. The president thought he could have offered a different perspective or at least lessened the impact if he had spoken directly to Woodward.

Why they didn't connect remains a mystery. It's possible that an aide, whom Woodward called, ran the author's interview request by the president, who said no. Sarah used to approach him with dozens of interview requests. There were times he declined all of them, and honestly, I didn't blame him one bit. Why waste an hour of his precious day doing an interview when the story was bound to be critical no matter what he said?

Then, a week later, a story would come out that wasn't good for us, and the president would ask, "Why didn't they ask me for a comment?"

"Sir," Sarah would tell him, "you said at the time you didn't want to do any interviews."

Another possible explanation was that the Woodward request might have been given to the president at the wrong time. Timing was everything with him. There were some items on my list that I would wait for a few days, if not longer, to run by him. I could sense when he was in the right frame of mind to deal with something and when he wasn't.

Or maybe the request had never been passed on to him at all. Who knows?

In any case, the president called Woodward to find out what had happened.

"Did you speak to Madeleine?" he asked.

No, Woodward said.

"Madeleine is the key."

★

The Woodward book told the public what was common knowledge in the West Wing: that the president and General Kelly weren't on the same page.

You know that discipline that was so necessary, to get everything in order after Reince left? Well, it was that same need for discipline, as General Kelly saw it, that led to his undoing. The general tried to run the White House as if it were a battalion, and that wasn't Donald Trump's style.

Nor, if you recall, was it his tendency to get rid of people. Instead, the two, like a husband and wife each waiting for the other to file for divorce, hung on for months: Kelly on the outside but not willing to resign; the president hoping every day that he would.

Not that the general didn't threaten to quit. He actually threatened to quit several times. "I'm out of here," he would say. "You're never going to see me again."

As he walked out of my office, I thought to myself: Okay, see you tomorrow.

Some days, he was as good as gone.

"Get the chief over here," the president would say.

I would call the chief's office and speak to his assistant. "The president wants to see the chief," I told him.

"Okay," the assistant would say. "I'll get him."

Five minutes later, the chief would have yet to show up. It takes about five seconds to walk from his office to the Oval.

"Where's the chief?" I would ask again.

"He's coming."

Only he wasn't coming, and now the president would be really agitated. I would head over there myself to find out what was causing the holdup.

"The chief is in a meeting," I would be told. "He can't be disturbed."

"Well," I would insist, "the president wants him down there right now. He has to come."

My plea would do absolutely no good. The general had refused a summons from the president of the United States. Incredible.

On other occasions, when the president complained that there were too many meetings on his schedule, General Kelly, in a childish fit, would go to the other extreme. "Okay, we'll schedule only one meeting a day," he'd suggest. "We will start at noon and end at two."

Then, when I would let him know that someone would be soon coming into the Oval Office, he'd respond, "I don't care. Do whatever you want."

I would be beside myself. First the general tries to run the West Wing as if it were another branch of the military, and now he doesn't care? What does that accomplish?

I wasn't totally surprised when, in late 2017, he had nearly come to blows with Chris Crane, the head of the National ICE Council, the union of officers employed by the Immigration and Customs Enforcement (ICE) agency, which monitors immigration and crime.

There was some history between them, that's for sure.

When the general had been secretary of homeland security, Crane had told the president that Kelly "is not giving us our people." The general had said it was a lie. The president, however, had continued to meet with Crane, as the border was a huge priority for him and his base. Once during a meeting with Crane and the president, Kelly, now the chief of staff, suddenly stood up and said, "I'm out of here."

Toward the end, when the president asked how I felt about General Kelly, I chose my words carefully. "This is probably no longer the right job for him," I said.

As toxic as their relationship had become, I couldn't be sure that it wouldn't, at some point, improve. The president had chosen the general for a reason, and that reason was still valid: to bring order to the West Wing. If they were to become on good terms again, I would hate to be on the record as having been anything other than totally supportive of the chief of staff.

I later made that mistake, by the way, when the president asked what I thought of Mick Mulvaney. "Mick's annoying," I told him.

Two weeks later, the president named Mick as Kelly's replacement.

Ooops.

As with Reince, I often found myself in the most awkward position. The general, my immediate superior, would tell me, "Don't let this person into the Oval," while the president, his boss—everybody's boss—would say, "I want to see this person."

I sided with the president probably 90 percent of the time, and I don't regret it for a second, although it caused problems between the general and myself. How could it not?

In December 2018, General Kelly resigned. No one was surprised. He'd been in the job for seventeen months, an eternity in the Trump White House. Reince had lasted just six months. Despite everything, I empathized with the general, as I had with Reince.

Only this time I wasn't worried about my future.

Reince had brought me into the West Wing. The general hadn't. I wasn't seen as a "Kelly person" by others in the building.

If anything, I was ready for a change. The speculation was that he would be replaced by Nick Ayers, the vice president's chief of staff. Nick and I were on excellent terms, with him even telling me that I'd be promoted and given added responsibility if he took the job. He trusted me and knew the president trusted me. As I'm sure it's clear by now, trust was everything.

Unfortunately, Nick didn't take the job. Which was how Mick Mulvaney wound up as acting chief of staff.

Mick tried to be lenient and easygoing, everything the general was not. There were numerous happy hours in his office and multiple trips to Camp David. A few of us called him "Chief of Fun."

He tried too hard, in my opinion. He was always practicing his golf swing and, like Lindsey Graham, jumped at every chance he could to join the president's foursome. He was, as I had told the president, "annoying." In the beginning, Mick was in the Oval Office every second. I remember thinking, *The president will get sick of this real fast.*

I will say this for Mick, though. He realized from the start that, title or not, he wasn't really the chief of staff. The president was. He also didn't try to limit the influence of Jared, Ivanka, or any other member of the family, as Reince and the general had. Which was why he stuck around for as long as he did.

Mick and I were on good terms. I don't blame him for forcing me to resign. He did what he thought was best to protect the president. That was his job.

# CHAPTER SIXTEEN

## The Search for Forgiveness

For months, whenever I thought of the dinner in Bedminster, which was at least once a day, I couldn't stop asking myself: What if?

There are almost too many what-ifs to mention.

What if I'd said no when Hogan asked me to join them the second time, as I had on the other occasions I was asked to spend time with reporters? I could have taken an Uber from Bedminster to my hotel, ordered room service for dinner, watched a movie, and gone to bed.

What if I'd attended the bachelorette party in Montauk? It might have been inconvenient to get back to DC on my own on Sunday morning, but it wouldn't have been impossible, and what a great opportunity and refreshing change it would have been to connect with old friends outside of the political arena. We would have laughed and celebrated the bride-to-be.

What if I'd taken Nick Luna up on the generous offer he'd made to step in for me the last couple of days before I left for

California for the surgery? I could have flown back to DC and hung out with Ben before I left. Nick had been more than willing to come up, and the president had plenty of capable people around him. I wouldn't have been missed.

What if I had pushed back on Daniel Lippman, the Politico reporter? Maybe he wouldn't have listed specific comments he was told I had made about Barron and Tiffany. It would have been too late to save my job, but I would have spared a great deal of embarrassment for myself, the president, and his family.

And finally, what if I had been in the West Wing when Mick found out about the dinner? If I had met with the president in the Oval Office, perhaps he would have seen how sorry I was and given me another chance. At the very least, I might have a better idea of how everything unfolded.

I could go on, but what would be the point? I would only be torturing myself, and I've done enough of that already.

Besides, I was much more interested in a different question, the one the president asked the day I apologized before he took off for Camp David: What happened?

For the longest time I continued to tell myself that I was trying to humanize the president, to share a side of him that not many people get to see and explain that he and his family, in some ways, are just like everyone else. I hadn't been able to think of any other reason why I was so careless.

After months of reflection, I see that there was more to it. I simply had too much to drink at the absolute worst moment to deal with all the stress I was constantly under.

The problem wasn't just talking to the reporters, as nerve-wracking as that was. It was also the pressures and demands of working in DC. I'm ashamed of the choice I made, but that is how so many people cope here. They work hard and play hard. I believe that almost everyone in this town can relate to having had an extra cocktail or two at an inappropriate time and suffered the consequences. My lapse in judgment just had the misfortune of playing out on a much larger stage.

All I know is what I said to my mom moments after I got off the phone with Mick. Still, literally, shaking from the call, I told her I was "kind of relieved." Not relieved to be out of my dream job. Heavens, no. I loved going to work every day and serving a president and working on an agenda I believed in. Rather, I was relieved to be out of the intense environment that encompasses DC, and politics in general.

Maybe it was because I had been in California for almost a week, and for the first time in a long time, I was relaxed, calm, and happy. I put my phone down, which I hadn't done in months, and didn't worry about checking my email every two minutes. I was enjoying downtime with my family. Imagine that.

Maybe it had something to do with the dinner, that I had known I would have to pay the penalty for what I had said and now at least the anticipation was over and I would no longer have to be afraid.

Or maybe it was related to a truth about myself I had tried to bury for the longest time: I didn't like the person that I had become while working in the White House. Simple as that.

I am not proud of the way I sometimes treated people. Not everybody, such as the president, the members of the cabinet and Congress, or the CEOs I regularly spoke with. I was respectful and friendly to them, having built strong relationships that dated back to my days as greeter girl. I built enduring friendships with many of my colleagues and those I interacted with on a daily basis. You can't get through the day in that kind of job without the support of others. I also enjoyed doing things for people, such as arranging a birthday celebration or bringing someone in to meet the president.

The ones I wasn't always kind to were at my level or below me. Take, for instance, the assistants to senior administration officials. They do so much of the work in this city and get so little credit. I should know. I was one of them.

The problem was that I was only used to taking care of the person at the top, starting with Katie Walsh at the RNC. So I had little experience dealing with other assistants telling me what would or would not work for their bosses. To me, it didn't make any difference, because my boss was the only person who mattered.

On occasion, I was condescending and just plain mean. When an assistant called to see if the president's meetings were running late or on time, I had no patience whatsoever. "Well, your boss's meeting with the president starts at three p.m.," I'd tell Stephen Miller's assistant, for example. "I don't know whether the president will be on time or not, but I suggest you have Stephen here at three. If he's running late, then Stephen will just have to wait."

Looking back, I can't help but wonder: What was my problem? Those assistants were only trying to do their job, just as I was trying to do mine. I could still have been strict while showing some compassion. The same goes for when I told people to stay out of the president's line of sight. I didn't have be so direct. The expression on my face was sometimes more telling than any words. When I heard the vice president say, "Oh, Madeleine's giving us the look. We better step out of the Outer Oval," I should have been mortified. I wasn't.

Even my mom noticed. She sent me books and articles on kindness, mindfulness, and gratitude. I didn't read them. I was too busy. She later told me that she was beginning to worry about the person I was becoming.

The sad truth is that I was fully aware of how I was behaving, and I still didn't change. I tried—at least I told myself I would try.

Many nights, when I got back to my apartment and away from the West Wing, I would make myself a promise before I went to bed: Starting tomorrow, I will be different. I will be nicer.

However, something would happen to set me off—an improper email, a stupid question, it could be anything, really—and I would be the same bitchy Madeleine, for at least another day. On lots of occasions, I was reacting to being inundated with requests for the president's time or someone blaming me for the schedule being too heavy when it wasn't my fault. It didn't take much.

Sarah Sanders used to tell others, "The person I'm the most terrified of in the White House is Madeleine." We got along great, and I consider her a true friend, but I don't think she was entirely kidding.

Even the president brought it up once, and it may very well have been the lowest moment during my whole time with him.

It was during his trip to Turnberry, the golf resort he owns in Scotland, in the summer of 2018. I'd gone there ahead of him, and on the first night he arrived, he was listening to some Scottish bagpipers when he spotted me standing off to the side with the Secret Service and members of the club's staff. I'm quite sure he hadn't realized I'd be there.

He walked toward me, and without stopping or even saying hello, was as blunt as ever. "You know why people don't like you?" he said. "It's because you are too short with them." That was it. He kept walking without saying another word.

I was stunned, and embarrassed. I was certain that others heard what he said. I went to the staff office and sat by myself for a few minutes, trying to process what had happened. It's quite likely he has long forgotten the entire interaction. I never will.

I was upset about it for the rest of the trip. Later on, we had a big dinner with the entire traveling team: the president's senior staff, the first lady's staff, the advance team, and the military aides. While everyone was sharing stories about the trip and laughing, I couldn't stop thinking about what the president had said to me. I finally got up and left because I didn't want anyone to see me cry.

Again I made a promise to myself: I will be kinder to people.

Yet I broke that promise over and over. I assumed that being tough on people was the only way I could do my job. Somehow I forgot that I hadn't gotten to the White House on my own. Many people had helped me along the way. Katie, Reince, Jared, Hope, Dan, the list is a long one.

I also seemed to forget that working in the White House wasn't a right, it was a privilege. As much as I saw myself as irreplaceable, there were countless other people who would have given anything to sit at my desk for just an hour. In fact, moments after Mick let me go, there were already people, according to his deputy, Emma Doyle, volunteering to "help out" in the Outer Oval Office.

Who knows? If I had stayed at the White House much longer, I might have become even harder on people. I don't like to think about it.

★

As time has passed, I have also had a chance to reflect more on the dinner itself.

For months, I blamed myself almost entirely. Whenever anyone, even Sean Hannity or Tucker Carlson, shifted the majority of the blame to the press, I felt very uncomfortable. I refused to be another person to shirk responsibility.

I see that night differently now. The press, and not just those at the dinner, was as responsible as I was. Check out this statement, which was in Daniel Lippman's piece in Politico, from the national editor at the *Washington Post* defending Phil Rucker, who was at the dinner:

> Philip Rucker is one of the best and most scrupulous reporters in the news business. He has always acted with the utmost honor and integrity and has never violated *Washington Post* standards or policies.

That might very well be true, but Rucker's reputation isn't the issue. The issue is: Did he, or anyone, share my off-the-record comments with anybody who was not at the dinner?

I have given a lot of thought, too, to Hogan's involvement. Why did he ask me a second time to go to the dinner? Having spent much of the day by the pool together, he had seen me have a few drinks. I'm not suggesting that Hogan was responsible for me, but as the deputy press secretary, maybe he should have known that I wasn't in the right state of mind to be dining with reporters.

Which brings up a larger question: Was someone in the White House, or even outside of the administration, out to get me?

I wouldn't be shocked. There were enough people who didn't like the fact that the president trusted me so much. I was an executive assistant, yet he asked me to do things well outside my job description, tasks often given to the chief of staff, not a secretary.

As Jennifer Jacobs, one of the four reporters at the dinner, put it in a tweet the day I was let go:

Knives out for Madeleine Westerhout for a while. . . . It's game of thrones at WH.

I wouldn't go quite that far, though Jennifer had a point. In any case, I'll never know what happened. I have just always found it convenient that I was out of the building when word got to Mick. It's much easier to get rid of somebody if they're not around to defend themselves.

★

As the months went by, I often thought about calling the president. I missed him so much. I even asked my former colleagues in the building if he would take my call. Yes, they said, he would love to hear from you.

Why didn't I call? It's simple, really. I knew he would ask how I was doing and what was going on in my life, but there was nothing to tell.

Finally, in early March, shortly after I went home to California, we spoke. I reached out to tell him about this book. I was sitting in the same exact spot, ironically enough, that I had been when I had spoken to him last, on that horrible Friday afternoon in September.

I was very nervous, knowing how he feels about people who write books after they leave the White House, and now I was one of them. The last thing I wanted was for him to think I was going to trash him, as so many others have done.

"Here we go, another book about Trump, another 'tell all' from someone who barely knows me," he used to say.

Fortunately, he couldn't have been nicer, wishing me well with the book and with everything else. When I hung up, I felt happier than I had since the day I left.

It occurred to me that the president had forgiven me back in September but I had still not forgiven myself. Although many people had said the president was not angry with me, I couldn't quite find a way to move on. It wasn't until I heard his voice again that I was finally ready to forgive myself and truly move forward.

The president and I spoke again a month later. That time, he reached out to me. Only moments before, he'd wrapped up a press briefing about the Coronavirus. With everything that had to be on his mind, the fact that he would take the time to call meant a great deal to me.

I believe he wanted to hear a friendly voice, to talk with someone who had been there for him before in tough times and knew the pressure he was under.

The virus was affecting the president on a personal level, as it was affecting all of us. His close friend Stanley Chera, a major real

estate developer in New York, was in the hospital in a coma, suffering from complications related to COVID-19. I'd been working
on some projects with Stanley and had just seen him at the end of
February. He was one of the kindest people I had met during my
time in the White House and had been so gracious to me after I'd
left. I'm not sure the president had a bigger fan or a better friend
than Stanley, who passed away about a week after the president
and I spoke on the phone.

Boris Johnson, the prime minister of England, whom he is
quite fond of, was also in bad shape.

During our phone call, the president reminded me of the
time I had reached out to Boris Johnson when it had become
clear that his party was going to win the election and he would
become prime minister. I happened to have Boris's cell phone
number in my contacts, so I was able to connect the two of them
directly. The president felt that Boris's victory was a validation
of sorts of his own unorthodox brand of leadership.

The president and I didn't talk long that afternoon, but he
said that I could reach out to him if I ever needed anything. He
also told me to come visit him. I said I would, at the right time.

Hearing the tender sound in his voice and how genuinely concerned he was for my well-being, I thought about the man himself. Not the president, mind you, the man. There is a difference.

The president has to display strength at all times—to the
American people, to our allies, and especially to our enemies.
Anything less, and those enemies will take advantage. We've
seen it over and over. The man, on the other hand, can show his
vulnerability, and that's an essential part of the Donald Trump
I know and love, and I don't care what the critics say. They don't
know him like I do.

For me, one example that stands out is what took place on June 14, 2017, which was, ironically enough, the president's birthday.

Around 7:00 a.m., a gunman opened fire on a group of Republican members of Congress on a baseball field in Alexandria, Virginia, a DC suburb, while they were practicing for the next day's annual charity game. Several people were injured, including House majority whip Steve Scalise.

That morning, when the president arrived in the Oval Office, he did all the things a president should do: He spoke to members of Congress. He addressed the nation. He reached out to the families of the victims.

Yet that wasn't what I'll always remember. Rather, it was what happened after he did all that. Around 1:00 p.m., he told those of us in the Outer Oval, "I'm going up. I'm done for the day."

John McEntee and I were stunned. The president never took off for the residence that early.

It wasn't that he was done working for the day. Hardly. He made more calls and, with the first lady, went to MedStar Washington Hospital Center hours later to check in on Congressman Scalise, who had been injured the worst.

It was that the president needed to be alone, to compose his thoughts. The critics out there would never imagine it was possible, but I believe he was deeply affected.

At the time, we could not be sure the congressman would survive. Thankfully, he has recovered. There is something very disturbing when a member of Congress is attacked by an American citizen while on a baseball field, and the president, I believe, was trying to come to terms with that.

President Trump had dealt with a painful loss earlier that year when William Ryan Owens, a navy SEAL, had become the first soldier to die on his watch. Owens had died during a raid in Yemen. I had seen a similar look in the president's eyes when he had welcomed Owens' widow and three children to the White House on the afternoon of his first joint address to Congress.

I'm sure that the president never expected to go through an entire term without a member of the armed forces losing his or her life in service to our country.

Still, when it did happen, not even ten days into his administration, he couldn't have been prepared for the feelings that came up. Who is? I will never forget how warm and sweet he was with those three young kids, treating them almost like his own. I hope that in the years ahead, as they get older, it will give them some solace, realizing their father is a hero and that the president of the United States was honoring him.

One other example keeps coming back to me is the president's reaction to the wildfires in California in November 2018. I traveled with President Trump as he surveyed the devastation that resulted from the Camp and Woolsey fires in Paradise and Malibu. It was heartbreaking.

We arrived at Beale Air Force Base, the air thick with smoke, and were greeted by Governor Jerry Brown and Lieutenant Governor Gavin Newsom. The president had made it clear that he didn't agree with how the state handled forest management, but it wasn't the time to bicker. We were one team now.

There weren't many residents to meet with in Paradise or Malibu. Everyone had been evacuated.

Yet there was one group who didn't have that option, the first responders.

The president spent a great deal of time with them. He hoped to understand how the fires had spread so quickly and what could be done to prevent this from happening again. He told them how proud he was and praised them for the remarkable job they had done.

People think he doesn't have compassion for those who have suffered. They couldn't be more wrong.

★

I have no problem walking down Pennsylvania Avenue these days and hanging out with friends who remind me of my past life. Without them, I'm not sure I could have gotten through those difficult times. They cried with me, laughed with me, and made it safe to vent whenever I needed to. They, along with my family, reminded me that there are people who love me regardless of where I work.

DC will always be a place that I cherish. It is where I truly matured, got my first job, fell in love, and experienced heartbreak.

So much has happened since I left the White House, and not just the COVID-19 epidemic. Part of me yearns to go back, to walk the hallways between the West Wing and East Wing, to hear that distinctive voice from the Oval Office, ready with another hysterical tweet: "Madeleine, bring your pad."

Another part says: No way! I start to feel anxious when I even think about it. I enjoy having a balanced life, and I'm not convinced that if I were to go back, I wouldn't slip back into my old ways.

During those early weeks and months I wondered: Who am I away from the White House? Away from Donald Trump?

I'm still trying to figure that out, but I know one thing: I am more than my job. I wasn't sure of that a year ago.

I also know who I want to be: the best friend, the best daughter, and one day the best mother and wife I could possibly be. I want to connect more often with my sister and grandparents and with friends I lost touch with because I thought I was too busy. I should never be too busy to reach out to the people who have been there for me, in both tough and joyous moments.

Spending more time in California over the past year, I have realized there is life outside of Washington, DC. As each day went by, I began to heal a little bit more. I have been reminded of how much it means to be with my family. It means everything. I needed to be away from that job—and that city—to really gain a perspective.

I have also realized that I am proud of myself for how I have handled the fallout of losing my job, with maturity and dignity. I took the actions that were right for me, regardless of what anyone else expected me to do. I know I am exactly where I am supposed to be.

On that Friday in September when I apologized to the president, I was very remorseful, and I still feel that way, knowing that I hurt people I care about, but I have finally found peace.

Am I completely over the dinner in Bedminster? No, and I wonder whether I ever will be. Even now, when I'm having a drink at a restaurant or bar, I worry that there might be a photographer nearby and people will see it as further proof: there she is, drinking again.

Truth is, I've never had a drinking problem. At times, I have used alcohol as a coping mechanism when I was depressed or overwhelmed, but since the dinner, I've learned to cope with my emotions in more healthy ways.

Not every moment, I understand, as urgent as it may seem at the time, should be treated as a crisis. These days, I take long walks, work out, read, and spend time with family and friends.

The dinner used to come up a lot in my dreams—more like nightmares, really. In one very vivid dream, I was back at my job, but again I said something that I shouldn't have said.

"I have no choice but to ask you to leave," the president said.

I woke up the next morning feeling a physical, gut-wrenching pain like the one I felt when I lost my job.

In another, the first lady wrote a letter to me about my drinking at a dinner at the White House. "You can't be doing that at our house," she wrote. "That is something only our guests can do."

Even if I put that night behind me, not everyone will. Which brings me back to that dark place I was in for so long.

Earlier this year I flew to Miami to help out a former colleague with fund-raising for some of her clients. One of the candidates asked about my background. No sooner did I mention that I'd been President Trump's executive assistant than it dawned on her who I was.

"You're the girl who said those things at that off-the-record dinner," she said. She then asked the same old questions. I had no choice but to give the same old answers.

Around the same time, Ben and I were at a birthday party for a friend. I was still extremely nervous about going anywhere in public, but this was a dear friend and I knew I couldn't avoid social interactions forever. Plus it would be a wonderful opportunity to show that I was doing okay. A young staffer whom I had met back in the fall approached Ben and said, "Wow, it was so good of you to stay with her after everything that happened." We were both appalled.

I now know, however, that the dinner won't haunt me forever, as I feared it would. Sean Hannity was right. One mistake will not define me. What will define me are the principles and values I choose to live by going forward, and I have years, God willing, to do just that.

I needed the past year to think about everything and process it, but it is clear now that I get to tell my story. No one else does.

I consider myself fortunate to have gone through so much at such a young age, and I am not referring only to the experiences, as fascinating as they were. I'm referring to the lessons I have learned—lessons people usually don't learn until they are much older.

The following quote from Hugh White, a senator from Tennessee in the early 1800s, says it all: "When you make a mistake, don't look back at it long. Take the reason of the thing into your mind and then look forward. Mistakes are lessons of wisdom. The past cannot be changed. The future is yet in your power."

I know who my friends are. I know what matters most to me. I know that being kind to people is more rewarding than any job. I know that judging people from what you hear on the news isn't fair to them, or to yourself.

There was so much about working in the White House I wish I could have better appreciated. I didn't often stop to really think how we were improving people's lives. I was focused on the next meeting, the next call, the next event.

"How was your day?" Ben would ask when I got home.

"It was really stressful," I'd tell him most nights.

Rarely did I tell him about or take in for my own benefit the magnitude of what I was witnessing. It never occurred to me that it wouldn't end on my own terms, and then it did.

Now, however, again with the time to reflect, I can fully appreciate the small way I was able to contribute to critical moments in our country's history. The experiences have helped shape me into the strong, confident woman I am today.

Speaking of Ben, it's still too early to know what the future will hold for us as a couple. We have had months to reflect on that, but the answers have not come easily. I suppose they rarely do.

The same goes for my relationship with God. In high school, I reconnected with my Christian faith. I spent a week at a Young Life camp, playing in the lake, singing worship songs and learning about Scripture. I was baptized at my church in Orange County and truly felt the presence of the Lord.

Then came college and DC, and I exchanged one God for another, worshipping power like everybody else who wants to rise up in politics. God wasn't going to help me get that promotion, so why bother going to Easter service, let alone giving my life to him?

Removed from that false God, I am taking a deeper look at what the Lord means to me. Reading *The Message*, a contemporary approach to the Bible, and waking up with a daily devotional have become parts of my new routine. I have finally read some of the books on gratitude and mindfulness my mom had sent me, as well as a few I have found on my own.

One book, *The Gifts of Imperfection: Let Go of Who You Think You're Supposed to Be and Embrace Who You Are*, by

Brené Brown, made an especially strong impression. It begins with this line: "Owning our story and loving ourselves through that process is the bravest thing that we will ever do."

I felt as though she was speaking to me.

God works in mysterious ways that aren't always clear to us. If I hadn't lost my dream job when I did and how I did, I might never have been given the opportunity to own my story and love myself, flaws and all, through the process.

★

I often think about the day the man from the White House counsel's office and the HR woman came to my apartment to give me the belongings from my desk and take back the items that belonged to the White House.

That day, I felt as though they had taken everything from me, but I was wrong. No one will ever be able to take away the memories I have of serving our country and a president I love and admire. Those memories are mine, and I will cherish them forever.

# Acknowledgments

There are so many people who helped to make this book a reality, and I am forever grateful to each one of them.

Thank you to my agent, WME's Mel Berger, who guided me throughout this unknown process and knew from our first meeting who would be the best editor to bring my story to print. His patience and professionalism are unmatched.

I owe a great deal to my editor, Kate Hartson, and the entire team at Hachette: Daisy Hutton, Patsy Jones, Sean McGowan, Katie Broaddus, and Eliot Caldwell. Thank you for working so hard to produce the best possible version of my story. Kate saw a clear vision for this book before I did.

I must give a special thanks to President Trump. The more than two and a half years I spent sitting outside the Oval Office were the most exciting of my life. I wish everyone could get to know him the way I did. They would never doubt how much he loves this country.

Not to be overlooked are former colleagues at the White House, many of whom became good friends—all of my Outer Oval officemates, cabinet secretaries, military aides, Secret

Service personnel, White House photographers, residence staff, valets, the Executive Support Team, agency staff, military personnel, and so many others. The tremendous experiences we shared will always be something I look back on fondly.

I could not have gotten through such a difficult time without the support of my friends, especially Cathy, Carrie, Lara, Mallory, Cara, and Bridget. They have reminded me that my own self-worth is greater than any job. Good friends are a true blessing, and I am so fortunate to have such a wonderful group from many different walks of life.

Likewise, I truly believe I would not have been afforded the incredible opportunities I've had without the mentorship of Katie Walsh. From my first day at the RNC, Katie taught me the importance of hard work, integrity, and grace. She is a brilliant political operative but, more important, a loyal friend.

As for my boyfriend, Ben, I know this past year was not what we envisioned for ourselves, but I so appreciate his support and encouragement while I took the time to heal in my own way, on my own time. His steadfast commitment to everything he values is one of the reasons I fell in love with him. I hope to share a lifetime of the highs—and the lows—with him.

I have been so fortunate, as well, to have such loving grandparents: Gammy, Mamu, and Grandpa. They have served as constant examples of wisdom and strength. Not many people are fortunate enough to have been able to grow up with grandparents; spending time with them and hearing stories from their incredible lives is something I have never, and will never, take for granted.

My sister, Katie, is someone else I cherish greatly. I love being the older sister, but I often look to her as an example of resilience and optimism. Her infectious laugh, even at seemingly inappropriate times, is a sound I hope to never stop hearing. I am lucky to have a built-in best friend in her and am so proud of the beautiful woman she has become.

And of course, my mom and dad, who always put Katie and me first and did everything in their power to provide for us. I'll start with Mom, who instilled in both my sister and me the understanding that we could do anything and be anything we put our minds to and the desire to dream big. She has cried with me when I was completely broken and provided the comfort only a mother can, and sent me countless books and messages on mindfulness, kindness, and spirituality. I am so grateful for her persistence. I hope she never stops sharing with me what she discovers in this fascinating world.

As for Dad, he has been an incredible example of what a balanced life can look like. I could not have asked for a better "girl dad" and someone who has championed me in everything I choose to do. He sat with me in silence when there were no more words to be spoken and made me feel safe and protected. I am so thankful to have him and my stepmother, Carrie.

Finally, I will never forget the kindness that so many people—old friends, former colleagues, relatives, and even strangers—showed me along this journey. I am forever humbled.